A Dialect Dictionary

When a farmer who has spent his life on the Derbyshire hills
– who also trained as a classical pianist – turns performance
poet, you might expect the outcome to be fascinating
and intriguing, especially when the communicator
has the lively wit, imaginative curiosity and
skill with words of F. Philip Holland.

This author cares deeply about people,
their lives and emotions, their thoughts and history.
Having written poems in the dialect of his native
village of Earl Sterndale, he became concerned
that the dialect spoken by his forebears
is fast passing out of use: subsequent research revealing
it will probably become obsolete within another generation.

This, he has pledged, both as a lover of words and
of the country life-style they represent, shall not happen.
But this book is more than just a record of the dialect
of a village and an area– it is a loving tribute to
the people of the White Peak, a personal crusade by
a man who knows and loves the land where his roots lie.

*'Philip's poetry is quarried from his Derbyshire, and flows with the
unconscious, natural speech rhythms…of this locality'*
Alyson Phillips

P. Holland.

2

Words of the White Peak

The Disappearing Dialect of a Derbyshire Village

F. Philip Holland

Anecdotes Publishing

ISBN: 9781898670 155
Text copyright © F. Philip Holland 2008
Illustrations copyright © Pat Holland 2008

Published by: Anecdotes
70 The Punch Bowl, Manchester Road,
Buxton, Derbyshire SK17 6TA

Printed and bound by:
RPM Print & Design, 2-3 Spur Road,
Quarry Lane, Chichester PO19 8PR

For further information go to
www.anecdotespublishing.co.uk

You can contact the author on:
www.fphiliphollandpoetry.co.uk
Email: info@fphiliphollandpoetry.co.uk.

Dedication

This book is dedicated to the memory of my grand-father Albert William Holland and my father Frank Edward Holland - who spoke all these words.

Thanks

To Patty, my dear wife, for her illustrations. No-one knows me better than she does, so there is really no need to tell her. Anyway, there are no words to say how much our life together means to me.

To my children, wider family and friends: they are the kind of people everyone should have in their lives. They know who they are.

To my dear friends Dilys and Paul Gater, who have supported and guided me throughout this publication. I am very grateful for their patience, hard work, artistic professionalism and their belief in me.

Poetry collections by Philip Holland:

Selected Poems (April, 2004, 2nd Ed. Aug. '04, 3rd. Ed. Jun., '05)
More Poems (June, 2005)
Poetry, Times Three (July, 2006)
Fourth in Line (July 2007)

This isn't a scholarly tome,
like a wild flower, it grew when it was ready.

The words are earthy, for which I make no apology.

Political correctness is something I choose to despise and ignore. Those people that live in rarefied circumstances possessing delicate constitutions, or that are too nervous to buy black puddings, or aren't prepared to "ketch 'owd!" had better put this publication down now. You have been warned; bluntness is always sharpest.

I could have waited another year or two before publishing this book, and certainly would have probably thought of more examples for the dictionary, but I'm getting relatively old and impatient, and anyway, I might start to forget some of the words I have included.

There are many words of my father's and even more of my Grand-father's, which are missing. Younger people are always guilty of not listening to or remembering all their elder's experiences and wisdom. When they want to clarify something or bring back some point of interest from times past, it is the old people who have to put them right

Any omissions in this dictionary are not intentional, however, they are regretted.

F. Philip Holland

Contents

Foreword
by Her Grace
The Dowager Duchess of Devonshire

This book has been written just in time. The richness of a fast disappearing vocabulary in what was once a remote area of the High Peak is very fascinating to people who are only accustomed to voices and words heard on radio and television.

I have lived in Derbyshire since 1943 and during those 65 years everyday words and phrases have been lost at an ever-increasing rate, partly due to the incredible changes in agriculture and rural life as a whole.

The words used to describe all to do with livestock and cultivating the land have vanished along with the implements and processes we knew in those far off days. How many remember hand-milking, hoe-ing, ploughing with one horse, its harness, stabling and all that was familiar before mechanisation? The crops, the work in the garden, the domestic details of coal-fired kitchen ranges are of another world.

It is wonderful that the results of F. Philip Holland's research and memories have been collected in this book to remind us of what has gone before.

June 2008

Acknowledgements

When our perils are past, shall our gratitude sleep?
William Pitt (the Younger)

I gratefully acknowledge the help and support given to me by: Mr & Mrs E. Armett; Mr F. Bagnall; Mr F. Belfield; Mr & Mrs W. Cartledge; Mr J. Chats; Mrs J. Cundy; Mr R. Dakin; Mrs J. Dalton; Mr & Mrs T. Dickon; Mrs M. Etches; Mr & Mrs D. F. E. Holland; Mrs S. Holland; Mr & Mrs J. Melland; Mr & Mrs R. H. Morten; Mr & Mrs W. J. Nadin; Mr & Mrs T. Naylor; Mr & Mrs D. Taylor.

Also by Bakewell Y.F.C.; Buxton Y.F.C.; Hope Valley Y.F.C. and The Farming Life Centre, Blackwell Hall, Taddington.

Special thanks go to my sister-in-law, Mrs Margaret Taylor.

And finally, thanks to Dr. Teresa Barnard and Diana Syder.

PHILIP HOLLAND – THE WRITER

by Dilys Gater

I first met the multi-talented Philip Holland – farmer, hotelier, pianist and poet – at the Buxton Festival Fringe in 2006, where we shared a venue for our separate events. He was giving a recital of *Philip, Poetry and Piano* and my husband Paul and myself were holding a launch for the book we had just published on the composer Sir Arnold Bax.

So what might be described as our first collaboration resulted in Philip (with characteristic generosity) offering the use of his Yamaha keyboard for our guest, the pianist David Owen Norris, to use at the launch. We attended Philip's show (his third at the Fringe, each featuring a new collection of his work), his 'relaxed, civilized event', as I described it later; and he came to our launch and saw David play two Bax piano pieces on his keyboard. That was the beginning of our friendship.

Paul and I were impressed at Philip's skilful performance of his own poetry as well as his expertly played piano accompaniment.

'Now we can begin to see the development of his own authentic voice,' one reviewer wrote, 'speaking about the things which interest him; the countryside as expected from someone who has spent the greater part of his life farming, music as also expected from a fine musician, but other sources as well...

'Philip reads his poems with a quiet confidence which is most attractive...A delightful way to spend an hour on a summer's day in Buxton.'

As a result of our meeting I interviewed Philip a few weeks later for the magazine of which I was Arts Editor. My feature was called *Man of Many Words*. I described how he had left Buxton College Grammar School at the age of 16 to work on the family farm in Earl Sterndale – which is a village in the Hartington Middle Quarter of North-West Derbyshire. After a life in hill farming he had retired and 'one might have expected he would want to put his feet up metaphorically.

'But then, Philip Holland is not your average farmer…'

To date his accomplishments include that of concert pianist (he studied with the celebrated Fanny Waterman of Leeds); competitive performer in the amateur theatre on a national level; hotelier (owning and running a country guest house in the Manifold Valley for fourteen years). He has completed courses in Creative Writing; has four published collections of his own poetry – and he has just completed a three year degree course in English and Creative Writing as a mature student at the 'Dome' Campus of Derby University in Buxton.

Philip also dared to venture to the Edinburgh Festival Fringe in 2005, where he performed three recitals; he has had poems shown at the Oxo Tower and Bargehouse on London's South Bank; and won Joint First Prize at the Huddersfield Literary Festival in 2006 with his moving and emotive poem *The Gather* about the death of his faithful sheepdog.

'For me,' he says, 'performance of the written word is the most vital and meaningful vehicle to bring fresh appreciation of poetry in all its forms and styles. To communicate and touch other people's lives, of all ages, through the printed and spoken word is one of my greatest pleasures.'

Philip has tackled all kinds of poetry – an intriguing mix of sonnets, ballads, rhyming and free verse on themes descriptive, dramatic, reflective and comic. His observations are witty and can be caustic as well as deeply touching. He has

12

also written short stories, a musical entitled *Jason and the Argonauts* and some twelve chapters of a fictional saga set in the area where he lived and farmed.

A true poet does not need the poetic form in order to release the springs that will refresh the heart and touch the soul. Reviewer Alyson Phillips wrote perceptively of Philip's work: 'The theme of natural change is celebrated with a sense of security about our place in time using contemplative, perceptive poems that make you respond with a wry smile of recognition or laugh out loud with shared appreciation and understanding...'

In this book, whether he likes it or not, Philip is penning some of his most poetic thoughts as he reminisces about the people, the ways – even the animals – who have been familiar to him. And like any true poet, he is through seemingly casual comment and reportage offering a place to stand in the middle of changing times, without either judgment or bias. His words are, like the hearth of a farm kitchen, somewhere to warm yourself, to gather your resources together for trials ahead; they provide a benchmark against which to measure values; hearty companionship to celebrate personal success and an unexpectedly gentle touch in moments of grief and tragedy. Philip is a man to walk with whatever the mood or the challenge, a voice that says it as it is – but also as it might be; someone who knows how to be quiet when the need is for silence.

I have felt it a privilege to work on the manuscript of this book as its editor, to examine and come to know its contents as its publisher. Philip writes of his village that: '...it isn't the prettiest or the most interesting...' Yet within the parish 'there is evidence of ancient lead workings, early 'pudding-pie' lime burning kilns and interesting stone circles of the ancient 'Beaker' people. There have been important findings from the Neolithic and Neanderthal eras. Roman coins, Monastic Granges, Civil War bullets, old pack-horse trails, an empty tannery, a disused mill and a small defunct cheese factory all speak of Civilisation's march of time. At one time there was even a poor-house...'

I found a similar collection of hidden treasures tangled together in this story of the voice of the people, abandoned along the way in centuries of living in this remote corner of Derbyshire. They are waiting to be mined within this dictionary – from the contracts of the Hiring Fair to the cooking of pigs' heads; the shame of bearing a 'chance-child' to the use of a 'drenching horn' in doctoring animals. Want to know about the origins of 'eating humble pie'? Why the carts bearing aristocrats to the guillotine were called 'tumbrils'? Just read on.

Philip's work is rich and relevant in the way that other poets and writers have been relevant in their association with the areas they loved and with which they have become identified. It is no coincidence that the first book he ever bought with his own money (and which he still possesses) was the *Collected Poems of Thomas Hardy*. Nor that he admits to being 'blown away' by the writing of D. H. Lawrence.

When I first opened the manuscript I was reminded of the work of the Shropshire author Mary Webb – here is the same insight into both the physical and spiritual lives of country people, written in highly poetic language with great beauty set alongside great starkness. Philip's work will also stand comparison in my view, with the work of another Derbyshire writer Alison Uttley. The relentless, ever-fresh progress of the seasons, the flickering of winter light and summer shade, the shames and sufferings, the compassion and courage of ordinary people with little 'book-learning' who yet heard solemn music in the storm and saw poetry in a flower – they are all here.

Dilys Gater
Anecdotes Publishing

INTRODUCTION

The inwards of each place may best be known by such as reside therein
William Lambarede.

This collation was originally begun as a short list to record a few of the local dialect words, descriptions and phrases used in one particular parish in The Peak District in Derbyshire - Earl Sterndale. The list grew into a 'Concise Dictionary' and also a memoir of my life and work there.

I have not explored a vast amount of historical, geographical or anthropological research concerning the place of Earl Sterndale. These can be found in books of a more scholarly exactitude which are housed in libraries suited to such academic reading. My main focus here is dialect, and with this in mind I have interviewed long-established inhabitants of the area; researched in the Local Studies Department in the Derbyshire County Library; but chiefly drawn on my own experience and memory of hearing, knowing and speaking this dialect in my everyday life as a farmer.

In addition to putting all these dialect words before most of the senior citizens of the parish for their verification (and also some additions) I conducted a survey/questionnaire of about 150 people within a 5 mile radius, between the age of 88 and 9 years of age, taking a random sample of 36 words, to ascertain the knowledge and usage of dialect. Diagrams included in the book give my results and findings, along with a list of those who assisted me, to whom I would like to express my gratitude.

I took as my inspiration and main influence that wonderful piece of literature, the *Dictionary of the English Language,* created by Dr. Samuel Johnson (1709 – 84). Although not born in Derbyshire, Johnson had very strong connections with the county. His monumental work, published in 1755, is still regarded as the epitome of classical reference, language gymnastics and whimsical wit. I have tried to emulate his inimitable mix of academia and creative writing in this record of the language of my life and occupation!

References

You will find it a very good practice always to verify your references, sir!
Martin Joseph Routh (1755 – 1854)

Some references in the dictionary, in brackets, are secondary, consolidating examples of authenticity and verification, and may be marked with any of the following initials:

S.P. – Samuel Pegge (the Elder) *'Two Collections of Derbicisms'* (written 1751 – 1796) Published 1896, O.U.P

L.D. – The Right Honourable Lord Denman *'The Reliquary'*, 1862 - 3, Vol.3 and 1863 – 4, Vol.2.

C.P. - Crichton Porteous, *'Dickie's Skull'* (1940) Derby University Library.

T.H. – Teresa Hooley - writing in various *'Derbyshire Countryside'* magazines: 1949, Vol.17, No.6, April – June, p.255 and 1949, Vol.17, No.8, October – December, p.305.

W.P.F. – W. P. Featherstone, *'Notes on Dialect in the Dove Valley area'*, 1978, in *'Derbyshire Miscellany'* – Derbyshire Archaeological Society.

R.M. – Rosemary Milward, *A Glossary of Household, Farming and Trade Terms from Probate Inventories*, (1986), Derbyshire Record Society, Service.

J.B. – Julie Bunting, various articles in *'Peak Advertiser'* newspaper; 29th September, 1997, 24th March, 2008 and 21st April, 2008.

A DIALECT DICTIONARY
DEFINITIONS, TERMS & PHRASES

With examples of pronunciation, use and interpretation

Approximately 360 individual dialect words are included here. Abbreviations: *n. - noun, v. - verb, adj. - adjective, adv. - adverb, etc.*

I shall prove these writings not counterfeits, but authentick, and the contents true, and worthy of a divine original.
Grew's 'Cosmologia Sacra'

Any anecdotes and reminiscences will hopefully serve to illustrate all the season's sights, sounds, smells, tastes and touches, bring an awareness of the daily round of work and play and share a few moments in the life and times of a hill-farmer.

A

ABIDE. v. To endure. "Ah canna abide 'im!" – I can't stand him!

AGEN. adv. Against. e.g. "Dunna goo agen 'im" – Don't go against him. (C.P. p.11)

ANGLEBERRY. n. A wart (see also below Worrybray), a parasitic growth on the undersides of cattle, occurring especially in summer. Grey and husky, resembling the fruit of hops, they can grow quite large in size, even to compare with the size of a raspberry, an apple, or, occasionally, even a small melon.

ANYROAD. *adv.* Anyway, however or anyhow. *Anyroad* may begin, or end, virtually any sentence, it draws attention to the speaker when he/she says "Anyroad" and then pauses for effect, or to gain silence for the bit of gossip following.

'APPEN. *adv.* Perhaps. (Yes, I know it's minus an 'h' and should really be in the 'H' section. To put it in dialect - " 'Appen yow'd 'a put it theer. Ar didna." – (Perhaps you would have put it there. I didn't.) The word *'Appen'* often begins or ends a questioning sentence of suspicious conjecture or narrow-minded wiseacredom.

AR. - Can mean I or Yes, - depending on the sense. - Pronounced as the letter *'r'*

AY. *n.* Hay. E.g. "He's working in the hay" would be said: "Ee's i'th'ay."

By comparison, just over the River Dove in Staffordshire – and what a boundary a river can make - this would be uttered: "Ay's i'th'ee"

Thus it follows that "He is in the hayfield" in Derbyshire dialect would be: "Ee's i'th'ayfeelt." Yet within the sound of a peal of church bells in the adjoining county we get: "Ay's i'th'eefaylt."

AYE. (pronounced "I") – Yes.

AYRSH'ORN LIP. *n.* Or more correctly Ayrshire Horn Lip. A common description which refers to the unfortunate 'cleft lip' congenital abnormality. The Ayrshire cow has a particularly fine pair of curling horns that grow out from the head, curve forwards, and then point upwards. The cleft lip can resemble such a geometric pattern.

B

BACKEND. *n.* Late Autumn. When the summer weather starts to cool and the days begin to shorten, the stoic observation of; *"It'll soon be backend"* - "It will soon be late Autumn" will always be pessimistically uttered.

BACKSWATH._*n.* When mowing a field of grass, the first 'swath' or 'pass' around the field was with the mowing machine, (whether horse-drawn or by tractor), being pulled in a clockwise manner round the edge of the field. With the horse, or tractor, and mowing machine not too close to the wall, the cutting blades pointing to the middle of the field. but leaving enough grass uncut near the wall for the 'backswath'. This had to be cut in an anti-clockwise manner, with the cutter-bar (reciprocating blades) or the later 'drum' mower (with centrifugally thrown blades), close to the wall or hedge.

So, firstly, the field would be cut in ever-decreasing circles for perhaps 5 or 6 full perimeter 'swaths' or passes towards the middle of the field. Then, depending on the regularity of the shape of the field, or any steep banks, comes the 'setting out' of the field in… 'sets', leaving the already-mown headlands.

The *'backswath'* was usually the last piece of grass to be cut, in case any stones had fallen off the boundary walls and were hidden in the grass. By leaving the potential of damage to the blades until the end, the *'backswath'* was always the most awkward cutting pass as that grass had been partly flattened by the very first 'pass' of the tractor wheels.

BADGING. *v.* Cutting the last narrow swath of grass nearest the wall or hedge with a scythe at haymaking time. (see also *Hacking* below)

BADLY. *adj.* Unwell, not in good, rude health, .e.g. "How art?" (How are you?) "Am badly." (I'm not very well)

BAKESTONE. *n*. Pronounced *bakston'*. A flat, cast-iron circular plate of about 12 to 16 inches diameter, with 2 flat lugs on either side. Placed horizontally across the open fireplace, spanning the tops of the oven and the boiler either side of any typical old kitchen cooking range. About a quarter of an inch thick these temporarily placed cooking plates were used for baking oatcakes, etc.

BANKERHAND. *n*. (pronounced *banker'and*) A tool made entirely of wood, with a short shaft only long enough for the hand to grip around, and with a very large rounded hammer-head. It was used by stone-masons. When chiselling stone the large head of this tool enabled the mason to concentrate on the cutting edge of the chisel blade, not the striking end. The size of the head of the bankerhand made it virtually impossible to miss hitting the chisel head.

BARM. *n*. (also spelt balm) Yeast. (For bread-making.)

BARNACLES. *n*. An appliance for restraining difficult, fractious animals. Made of iron, resembling the size and shape of a human index finger and thumb with their tips touching to form an "O". A hinged base opposite these tips enabled the appliance to open to a "U" shape. At this hinged base is a short shaft with a strong spring wrapped around it. The 'opened' set of barnacles is applied to the septum (in between the nostrils) of the animal to be restrained, and the spring is released to keep the tips of the barnacles tightly fastened to the septum. A short piece of rope attached to the hinged base may be held by hand or tied to a post.

The similarity of marine barnacles sticking tightly to the undersides of ships and bovine barnacles gripping tightly to the animal is obvious.

(Also *'Bulldogs'*, see below.)

BAWK.(baulk) *v*. Literally 'baulking', by getting in the way of someone. Also (*n*.) small strip of grass left uncut at haytime, which when the hay or silage grass is cleared look rather embarrassing to the mower of the field! To leave 'bawks' may

21

have been because the grass was overgrown or flattened by heavy rain. But like an unprofessional haircut, there's only a week or two between a bad one and a good one. Also, *n.* The haylofts. (*Bulk*, S.P., p.9., also J.B., 1997.)

BAWLING. *v.* The sound of cattle either: in their 'heat', when their calves have been taken away from them, or when they are hungry.

BEASTINGS. *n.* The rich, thick, deep-pink or orange-coloured colostrum milk produced in the first few days by the cow after calving. A kind of custard made from *beastings* was considered quite a delicacy. It was simply put in a shallow dish, baked gently in a warm oven; it then thickens naturally, and is served either hot or cold, often with caster sugar or grated nutmeg on top. Some people referred to it as 'cow pie'.

BEESE. *n.* Cattle generally, - (pronounced as in 'geese') e.g. "*Fetchbeesewut?*" is "Will you go and get the cows in?" i.e. A typical form of composite phrase minus some words.

BELDERING. *v.* The bellowing (especially) of a bull. (see also *blorting*)

BELLAND. *n* . Land close by old lead workings, and thus contaminated from the spoil heaps. The old men used to say that; "*Tha munna put 'osses ont' belland. It's gyet a blue cyast on it in'th early mornin' mist. Youn pieson 'em.*" (You'll poison them.) Often trees were planted around these walled off areas, to suppress grass growth and minimise potential threat to grazing animals. Also, (*adj.*) the *actual* poisoning (bellanded) of stock by either grazing in close proximity to, or drinking water contaminated by leeching from, the spoil heaps of lead mining enterprises. (Rt. Hon. L.D. 1862 – 3 Vol.3, p.116.)

BELTING. *v.* Cutting away the dirty wool from the rear end of sheep , especially prior to shearing, or even at any time the flock is grazing lush, rich or overlong pasture. Not the most pleasant job, but no worse than changing nappies.

BIRD-NESTING. *v.* The old practice of young country lads searching for wild birds eggs in Springtime. Nowadays an illegal activity, in my early youth it was a common hobby, frowned on, but not of an environmentally sensitive issue in those days. Peewit (Green Plover), Woodpigeon, Curlew, Moorhen, Mallard, Pheasant, were all 'harvested' for the table. Young lads would only take one egg from a 'seen nest' of songbirds, i.e. one where the 'clutch' was still being laid.

Once fertile - ('Bird-ta'en' or 'Bird-tame', i.e. in the incubation period,) no eggs would be removed. Pricking a hole with a pin at each end of the egg, piercing the yolk and mixing it up with the white into a thinner consistency, and then gently 'blowing' the contents out resulted in a perfect specimen for a prized collection, usually set in cotton wool in an old biscuit tin. A collection of fifty or sixty different species was not uncommon.

The spraying of the profiteering chemical companies pesticides, (e.g. D.D.T.), various Government diktats on sheep-dips and warble-fly control did much more damage to wildlife than ever '*Bird-nesting*' did, - which had gone on for centuries previously. The twice-a-year slaughter of migratory British birds by the French, Italian and Spanish for the table, or to protect certain crops, is of far greater concern; Culture and Conservation often collide.

BLACK LEAD, *n.* Put onto the cast iron ranges, fire irons and fenders of the kitchen, it was a black, greasy composite polish containing graphite. Applied with a soft cloth then polished off with a small stiffish brush to produce a satanic, high-gloss finish. A never-ending fight against water splashes, cooking smears, soot, steam, ashes and coal dust, and born of a stubborn desire to keep yourself busy at all costs. Though I never recall a prize being awarded for the '*Shiniest Grate*'
A filthy task of little use but to stop the grate rusting and to make interminable washing. Whilst acknowledging this was a universal practise, it stayed on in the remoter countryside far longer than elsewhere. My sister-in-law, Mrs. Margaret Taylor of Wormhill Old Hall, admits to still using black lead today.

BLARETING. *v.* (also Blarting) The bleating of sheep.

BLORTING. *v.* The noise made by cattle when distressed either from hunger or perhaps when 'in heat'. (W.P.F., p.119.) N.B. *Blarting, Blorting* and *Beldering* (see above) are all similar, yet all subtly different.

BOGGART *n.* A 'Will o' the Wisp.' - Fabled 'fairy-folk.' Spirits living in wet, marshy ground, such as The Knabbs field. Which, incidentally, although <u>now</u> in Staffordshire, <u>was</u> in Derbyshire for most of my life up until the ever contentious 'Boundary Re-drawings'. N.B. Boggarts are not often seen there nowadays; Staffordshire Boggarts being much rarer!

BOG-SPAVIN *n.* extra lugs fitted onto wheels of farm implements to spread weight in wet land or wet conditions, and thereby dissipate the sinking in effect of narrow-wheeled rims. A *spavin* is also a growth in the middle of a horse's hoof.

BONNY-RAKE *n.* A wooden-hafted hand-pulled rake. At 'haytime', after the crop had been taken into the barns and haylofts, the field was raked over by a much larger, horse-drawn, two-wheeled rake to gather up the missed bits. Then, some particularly thrifty farmers would rake the field again with the smaller, closer-tined 'bonny-rake' for the very last wisps. *'Waste not, want not.'*

BONT. *n.* (or Bond) Baling-string especially, or any twine generally. (see J.B., 1997.)

BOOSE. *n.* The lying space in-between the two *boskins*, (see below.) Cattle were usually tied up in 'twos', sometimes the cowshed dimensions dictated one single slightly larger 'boose' at the end of a run of 'doubles', usually reserved for the largest animal, or a 'dry', pregnant cow, or even the bull.

BORSEN *adj.* (alt. Borsendt, Bossend), Very fat. An insulting adjective of a grossly overweight person. (W.P.F., p.117.)

BORTLED UP. *adj.* (or Borted up) – Very dirty, both farming attire and animal hides. Covered in muck. (W.P.F., p.117.)

BOSKIN, *n.* (or Bosgin) The wooden (later concrete) partition between 'stalled' (i.e. tied up by the neck) cattle. (R.M., p.9, also J.B., 1997.))

BOUK. *n.* (pronounced *bowk.*)A bucket or pail. Also an encouragement to eat up your meal. "Cum on, fill thi' bouk!" (J.B., 1997.)

BRANGLESOME. *adj.* Quarrelsome, unsavoury, vexatious.

BRAT *n.* A large piece of thick coarse sacking, usually an old Hessian meal sack, worn like an apron, but hanging at the back. Worn in severe weather when working outside e.g. thinning turnips, hedging, or *gapping* (see below), - to keep the lower back and hips sheltered and warm whilst standing or bending.

BRAWN *n.* Made from the pig's head. Initially, the cheeks, or *chorl* (see below) are sliced from the severed head and used separately. (*Chorl* is a separate delicacy, - as are the brains.)

The head, including all bone, is chopped with a cleaver into rough pieces about the size of a small apple. This is then vigourously boiled for an hour, or more, in a large pan, with some seasoning added, until the meat comes away from the bone and the water reduces to a grey, thickish gravy. Next, the bone is then removed, and all the meat mashed altogether. It is then transferred to pot basins, and allowed to cool and 'set' naturally. Covered with either grease-proofed paper or muslin it will keep quite a while. It is served warm or cold on bread or toast, much like a pate, carved or spooned.

Usually eaten with mustard, to either augment or disguise the taste. Not for the faint-hearted.

BRIM. *v.* (coarse slang.) *To brim, brimmed.* – Breeding, or the *actual mating* of pigs. On small holdings that couldn't, or didn't want to, keep a boar, then any sow 'on heat' would be temporarily transported to a larger farm that did have the required male pig. (S.P. p.8.)

There runs the old tale of the smallholder who took his sow to the larger, neighbouring farm that kept a prize boar at stud. As it was some distance, and he didn't want to upset the sow in her heat by walking her there, he loaded the animal into his wheelbarrow. Unfortunately, after the visit to the boar the sow didn't become pregnant.

At the next appropriate time the farmer took the sow back to the boar in his wheelbarrow again. Again, the sow failed to conceive. Some time later, the farmer's innocent young lad came running up to him.

'Eh up, Feyther, cum 'ere! Thez summat rum guin' on, th'owd sow's climbt int' th'barrer, 'er lukes az if shay's smilin'.'

BRIZZED. *adv.* Very cold, frozen. The phrase could be; 'Ah'm fair brizzed.'- 'I am really cold.'

BROODY. *adj.* The tendency of poultry to begin to sit on their eggs in order to hatch a clutch. If egg production was the financial reason for keeping poultry, rather than meat or breeding purposes, it was the practise to keep removing eggs from the nest-boxes, thus discouraging the 'broody' state. A hen wanting to go 'broody' stops laying eggs and will not readily leave her nest. She will fluff up her feathers and emit low, continuous cacklings rather than indignant squawks! One of my father's remedies to dissuade hens from this uneconomic, temporary condition was as follows. An old oil drum would be cut in half, and one half filled with water about two inches deep. The 'offending' hen would be dropped unceremoniously inside and covered over with an old sack. Obviously the hen would not sit down in the water, and after half a day a day or so would be 'knocked-off' broody! Another method was a 'broody coop', - a small wooden coop on legs with a slatted wooden flooring. The uncomfortable and cool conditions for a couple of days soon persuaded the hen to stop wanting to sit tight on eggs and to start laying some again.

BROW. *n.* Pronounced *'Broo'*. A bank or hillside.

BUCK-PLOUGHING. *v.* The practice of ploughing 5 or 6 passes across a field then ploughing the next 5 or 6 the other way, thus throwing the middle of the ploughed strip into a slight mound. The adjacent piece is then ploughed 'away' from this mounded area, thus forming a slight hollow, whilst the next piece over again is ploughed 'to' thus making 2 long mounded areas. the system would be continued over all the field. After discing, harrowing and rolling the finished result is like corrugated paper.

The idea was to increase the surface growing area of the field to increase production without having to purchase any more linear acreage. After many years of the field being ploughed repeatedly in such a manner, the mounds and hollows were exaggerated to such a degree the surface area of the field could be increased by 20, 30 or even 40%. The added bonus was slightly better drainage if the mounds and hollows ran up and down a slightly sloping field. The field drains were obviously put in underneath the hollows.

BULLDOGS. *n.* A set of *'bulldogs'* is another name for a set of *barnacles.* (see above.)

BULL-STONE. *n.* Pronounced "bullston'." A sharpening tool, compositely made from carborundum, tapered at both ends, about 12" long. Especially used for sharpening scythes (see also 'whetston' ').

BUN. *adj.* (or *'bun-up'*) Constipated. However, not always appertaining to internal inaction. Young, baby lambs can often accumulate a mass of congealed faeces around the tail area due to overly-rich colostrum from the ewes. This sticks and hardens to the nether regions of the lambs' fleece and prevents normal defecation, which, if unchecked over a week or so, can cause slow death.

BURLING. *v.* Cutting away the dirty wool from the nether regions of sheep prior to shearing. Similar to *Belting, (see above.)* *Burling* is the term more commonly used over in the Hope Valley area.

C

CACK. *n.* Excrement.

CACK-HANDED. *adj.* Clumsy, awkward, impractical, - especially with tools.

CAD. *n.* An eye patch.

CADE. *n* An orphaned lamb. (T.H., Vol.8, p.305.) Usually in the care of the patient farmer's wife, or the initially-excited, then later-unwilling, farmer's children. These cade or 'spare' lambs sometimes cannot be fostered onto those annoying sheep that rather un-sportingly only produce one lamb of their own, as the sheep will not accept them. (The unfortunate stepmother/step-child syndrome?)

Cades rarely thrive with the same vigour of naturally suckled lambs, and are a continuous drain on the resources of expensive milk substitutes and time. However, it's always good to have a few cades about you during lambing time to foster, and 'mix-and-match' the 'singles and triplets', replace 'accidental deaths' and thereby even out the ewe-to-lamb ratios. However, when the last ewe has lambed it's even better to have no cades left. The ideal sheep family is 'one ewe, two lambs'. For those who don't know, a ewe only has two teats, not like a cow which has four.

You may deduce from my various comments on sheep that I always preferred the dairy cattle; unless I had been kicked by a rather stroppy heifer in the milking parlour!

CALLING. *v.* The mealy-mouthed, derogatory insinuations by one person about another, - usually with the former out of earshot of the latter. The reciprocal description of the former being well-known for his caustic remarks by the latter would be, *"He's allis callin' some'dy!"* i.e. He is always 'bad-mouthing' somebody. This remark obviously well out of earshot of the former also. (T.H., Vol.8, p.305.)

CAMBRELL. *n.* A slightly bowed length of stout wood, (about the dimension of two cricket bats joined together without the handles), with carved ratchet-like 'teeth' on the top edge. There was usually a metal hook secured on the top , in the middle, to suspend the cambrell. Used to hang carcases on when being split into 'sides' of meat. The directionally-opposite-pointing 'ratcheting' on the upper edge allowed the legs to be held ever wider apart as the cleaver, or meat-saw, was used to split the carcase down the middle.

Also made from metal, and, later still, from stainless steel.

CANTING. *v.* Similar to *Calling* (above) Usually said with the added 'tales'. Spreading lies, revealing secrets, generally defamatory statements. "He's orlis canting tales abairt summat!" – He's always spreading the worst about something or somebody.

CAPON. *n.* A castrated cockerel. The neutering was usually achieved by chemical implantation of hormonal pellets implanted into the back of the neck of the young cockerel, thus aiding growth promotion without male aggressive tendencies: the fat eunuch syndrome!

CARR WATER. *n.* The dark reddish-brown water that drains off the peat moors and sandstone 'brows' into ditches from the Staffordshire side, and finally into the river Dove, - that being the county boundary between Derbyshire and Staffordshire.

CATER-CORNER. *adv.* (or *Cater-cornerwise*). Putting some-thing across a corner, i.e. as in the same place as the hypotenuse in a right-angled triangle. E.g., in the farming sense, this could be placing bales of straw to blank-off a corner to make a temporary triangular pen to hold a new-born calf within , or, by blanking off the corner, to stop young chickens crowding *into* the corner and thus possibly smothering each other. Cater-cornerwise might imply diagonally bracing a wooden frame, or, in a domestic sense, even placing a piece of furniture diagonally across the corner of a room for a more aesthetic effect.

CAWVING: *v.* Calving. There is often a losing of the 'L' consonant sound in much of Derbyshire's Dialect, e.g. *cowd* for *cold*, *gowd* for *gold*, *towd* for *told*, etc.

CESS. *n.* A portion of hay cut with a hay-knife from out of a 'loose' (i.e. not baled) haystack. (see also *'lap'* below.)

CHAIN-HORSE. *n.* The nefarious dealing between an unscrupulous Seller and an equally roguish Buyer to artificially push up the price of stock or goods at an auction. It works thus; The Seller takes his animal to market and knows, roughly, what he might make of it at auction. A Dealer spots an opportunity to make a little on the side. The Dealer suggests to the Seller he will buy the animal before the auction for a fair price. The Dealer may know of market forces the Seller is not privy to, e.g., this kind of animal is commanding a premium that particular week. The Seller senses his animal might make more than the Dealer is offering, as he is so keen to buy before the auction and on his terms. The seller would be happy with the price but sees an opportunity. One or the other suggests a 'chain-horse'.

The animal is put through the auction. The Dealer 'runs' the bidding quickly up to his pre-offered price. He was prepared to give this anyway, and the Seller would be fairly content also. If the animal is sold to him at the bid price, both parties are fairly satisfied. Should the animal make a much higher price and be sold to 'Another Party', then the Seller splits the 'profit' (i.e. that which is over and above the 'agreed' pre-auction price) 50/50 with the dealer. Thus, the Dealer gains a small 'fee', The Seller gets a higher price, less the 'fee' The Auctioneer gains a higher commission, The 'Other Party' pays a price he was prepared to give anyway. It's not absolutely honest, but the unofficial line in any market situation is 'Caveat emptor'.

Also; The chain-horse is the one in front of a team of horses that pulls first and 'sets the pace'. The similarity with the auction is obvious.

CHANCE-CHILD. *n.* An illegitimate baby. The term could be uttered disapprovingly or compassionately depending on the sensibility of the speaker, or the proximity of such a one to their own family. Sadly, some acid-tongued gossips would often use the term with relish and concentrated regularity about such a misfortunate, such abuse occurring to take attention away from their own questionably virtuous parentage.

CHAP. *n.* Pig's cheek, a culinary delicacy. (see also *'Chorl'*).

CHARLEY. (–on-'is –back). *adj.* Hump-backed, or crooked-backed. (see W.P.F., p.124.)

CHATTER. *n.* Low-grade, mixed-size, 'crusher-run' limestone, with a percentage of soil or clay, that is ideal for making rough farm roads, or as an initial base hard- core for all roadways or building construction. The clay helps to 'bind' and 'set' this aggregate, after heavy rolling, to consolidate it. 'Clean' stone, i.e. graded or washed, is not nearly so effective. (see W.P.F., p.121.)

CHEEKING. *n.* That part of a dry-stone wall which is built either immediately next to, but not touching, the two stone, or wooden, gate-stumps of a gateway into a piece of land, or up to a building. With plenty of *'throughs'* (see below) and large *'wall-ston'* (see below)' a well built *cheeking* is a very pleasing piece of craftsmanship.

CHELP. *n.* Cheek or rudeness, especially from ill-mannered children. Answering back would be referred to as *'Chelpin' back.'*

CHILDER. *n.* Children. *Childer-work* would be an accusatory remark for an adult's childish or immature behaviour.

CHOMMERED. adv. Land or ground just inside a field gate, which in wet weather becomes badly *'poached'*, i.e.

churned up, by the concentration of animals or machinery going through the gateway regularly.

CHOOSE-'OW. (Choose how) A composite expression put at the end of a sentence re-enforcing inevitability. Really meaning it wouldn't matter what one did, the outcome would be the same. (*D.S. p.2)*

CHORL. *n.* (Chawl) Pig's cheek. An epicurean delicacy, see also *brawn,* above. (W.P.F. p.117.)

CHUNNERING. *vb.* Mumbling disagreeably, but not really wanting to be heard.

CHUNTERING. *vb.* Similar to *chunnering.* (T.H. Vol.8, p.305).

CLAP POST. *n.* At a gateway, the post which the gate swings to, NOT is hung from. That would be the hanging post.

CLARTY. *adj.* Sticky, dirty, (J.B., 1997.)

CLEANSING. *n.* The afterbirth, placenta.

CLEM. *v.* To *clem, Clemmed* - Withhold feed from fattened stock prior to slaughter, or also *clemmed* - stock that is in poor condition through inadequate pasturage. *Also* to describe someone who is too thin, " Ey lukes clemmt' death!" (*Clam,* - Rt. Hon. L.D. 1863 – 4, Vol.2, p.16.)

CLENCH. *v.* To hammer sideways the points of any too-long nails that have been driven through a shallow piece of timber. (see W.P.F., p.124.)

CLIPPET *n.* The small "U"- shaped piece of iron hammered to the underside of the heels of leather boots or clogs to prevent wear and aid grip. A human horseshoe!

CLOSE. *adj.* Thundery weather, humid and oppressive (see 'Glooming') The expression would simply be – "It's close."

CLUSMPT. *adv.* (Clusumped) - Hands very cold, no feeling in fingers. "Ee! ahm clusmpt !" – Oh!, my hands are frozen.

COB. *v.* To throw.

COCKLOFT. *n.* Small space just under the roof, usually reached by ladder, even above an attic room or the highest garret. (R.M. p.15)

COLLAR-PROUD. *adv.* Describing a 'work-shy' person, one who dodges duties or makes excuses to avoid labour. Comes from a time when a horse might fidget or *'frab'* (see below) when having its collar put on after not working for some days. This might have been because of adverse weather or ground conditions. At any rate, anyone returning to work after a short holiday break, or illness, will appreciate the term readily. 'Back to the grindstone' would be a similar nuance.

COLLOP. *n.* A thick slice of something – bread, bacon or ham. (J.B., 1997.)

CONNA. *v.* Can't, cannot. "Tha conna 'a mine!" – You can't have mine.

COPER. *n.* The large, topmost stone of a dry-stone wall. Slightly rounded on the top, flatter across the base, These are positioned in a continuous tightly-packed line along the top. Sometimes upright, sometimes slightly leaning against each other. (W.P.F., p.124.)

CORVES. *n.* Calves.

COS. *v.* Can, (as in a question) Can you do it? - "Cos duit?"

COSSED. *v.* (pronounced "Cost") Told off with foul language, cursed. "'E cossed 'im." - He cursed him.

COW CHAIN. *n.* The chain that held the cow securely around the neck during stalled housing in the *shippons* in either winter time, or at 'milking time' in the summer months.

CRAW-BUN. *adj.* Gagged with food, in need of a drink to 'wash it down.' A composite word from *craw*, or *crop*, (the gizzard in poultry) and *'bun'*, as in bound tight, unmoving – see *'bun'* above. Might help to explain the phrase "It sticks in my craw that…." – It annoys me that……

CRIPPER-GAP. *n.* A smallish built gap in a dry-stone wall. Roughly 18" to 24" wide, and about 1 yard or so high. With properly built *'cheekings'* (see above) and rough, stone lintels these small apertures allowed sheep to *'creep'* through the walls from one field, or hill, to the next. It was a way of allowing the animals access between different grazings where it was impractical to form a normal, wide gateway because of land gradients, or cost, dictated so.

Also used to allow young lambs to get at the better grass first in a rotational form of grazing, before the older sheep were allowed access. Also to let sheep graze on steep, rocky land that was unsuitable for cattle.

To stop the passage through the gap you could either put in a couple of stout wooden stakes temporarily, or simply lean a small half-door against the gap propped to by a couple of large stones. Alternatively known as 'creep-holes'. (See also *"Smoose-holes"*)

CROW-QUEEGLER. *n.* A stone placed amateurishly on top of the line of coping-stones, i.e. not built in properly. Crows will often alight on these higher, unsteady misplaced stones, which will then rock from side to side, or *"queegle."*

CROZZLED. *adj.* Dried-out, burnt up, withered. Especially coal that 'welds' itself into an almost congealed or fused state as it burns. (see J.B., 1997.) Can apply to anything really, whether animal, vegetable or mineral. Even a spoiled or neglected meal left conspicuously on top of the 'Aga' by the exasperated distaff member of the family, fed up with waiting for the men-folk to come in for their meal, and therefore finally gone off to the W.I. meeting.

D

DANDY. *n.* A metal two-wheeled milk-churn trolley with a cranked, 'T' shaped handle at the top for the hands to either push or pull the appliance along. There was a hook near the top to hold the milk-churn on (by one of it's two handles), and a fixed half-hoop near the bottom, just in front of the wheel's axle, to steady the churn when in transit.

DERBYSHIRE NECK. *n.* Goitre. A medical condition not seen nowadays. Caused by a lack of iodine in the natural water.. Treatment of the mains supply eradicated this unsightly affliction.

DOCTOR GREEN. *n.* Literally, 'grass day' or letting the cattle out to pasture in Springtime. After being inside all winter, tired of being on straw bedding, standing on concrete areas and eating dry hay or pickled grass as silage, the natural diet and freedom of movement in outdoor grazing was the much needed tonic from Winter feed and housing.

DOG-HANGING. *n.* An event of great, some or little importance. The phrase might be:
" 'E goes ter iv'ry dog-hanging thur is." i.e. He doesn't like missing anything.

DOG-IN-A-MANGER. *n.* A mean or miserable person who has no use for something, but will not allow another, who could make use of it, to have that advantage. Like the actions of a spoilt child with too many toys, or a miserly, wealthy, very old person. Stems from the fable of the dog that made its home in a manger, would not allow the ox to come near to feed, and yet would not eat the hay in the manger itself.

DOLLY-TUB. *n.* The galvanised pressed-metal washtub. (see *Dolly-peg.*)

DOLLY-PEG. *n.* A pine implement used to '*Dolly*' clothes on washday. About a yard high with a cross-member handle near the top for both hands to grip. At the base was a circular piece with 5 or 6 pegs sticking out. On washday the *dolly-tub* was filled with hot water from the '*copper*', soap and the dirty linen were added. The dolly peg was plunged in, swirled left and right, lifted out and re-plunged again and again until the washing was completed. Next came '*mangling*', then hanging out on the clothes line, or '*winter-hedge*', or a final drying in front of the open fire if it was a wet day. Ironing with '*flat irons*' heated on the range completed this most laborious chore of laundry.

DOORBANDS. *n.* Iron straps either bolted or nailed across a door to support it on the metal 'hanging pins' driven into the door-jambs.

DONKEY STONE. *n.* Regular, 'soap-bar' shaped pieces of chalky material, which when dipped in water and rubbed on smooth masonry gave a decorative, 'whitening' effect. Used on window-sills, door-jambs, the 'risers' and sides of stone steps, etc.

Also used to make geometric patterns of swirls and curls around the stone-flagged hearth-place. When the patterns were worn they were scrubbed off, and re-applied ad infinitum. Another example of the love of labour. They were made by crushing soft stone and adding sufficient water to the fine dust to make a toothpaste consistency. this was then poured into small moulds and allowed to set . The Donkey-stones were then dried out. They were sold by general provision merchants and also rag-and-bone men. I often wonder if there was not just a hint of something slightly 'pagan' or 'warding off the evil eye' about the practise. In a similar vein to horse-brasses on the cart-horse? Though the exhibitors of show-harness on shires might disagree. (see *Horse brasses.*)

DRAWING. *v.* When maiden heifers have been 'put to the bull', after about five or six months into their pregnancy, it is possible to 'draw', by hand, or rather fingers, a very small amount of thick, clear, gluey secretion from the teats. This was a time-honoured method of confirming the animal was 'in-calf'. (This was before ultra-sound scanning made its debut.) Although once commonly practised, it is frowned on today, in that the 'seal' into the mammary system is breached, allowing possible infection of mastitis into the otherwise sterile udder.

'Drawing' cattle was a quick way of identifying any barren heifers or '*martins*' (see below), which could then be fattened for slaughter. The expression would be "They've all drawn in-calf."

DRENCHING-HORN. *n.* A mature cow's horn that has been cut off, hollowed out, and used as an ideal drencher for animal medicines. It is the right shape, angle and holds enough.

DROPPED-ON. Surprised. Taken aback. E.g. "Ah wur raight *dropped-on* when 'e towd me." – I was so surprised when he told me.

DROPPED LEATHER. *v.* To become very angry with someone. Probably comes from the ancient act of striking an adversary with a gauntlet, or glove, and throwing it down. If the struck person 'picked up the gauntlet' they were accepting the challenge to fight.

DRUGGETS. *n.* Long, white strips of cloth put on top of carpets, especially in hallways and on stairs, to take the brunt of wear. Freshly laundered druggets were put down, usually on Monday mornings, and taken up at the weekend, - when guests might call, or had been invited! A left-over prudence from Victorian days.

DUS. *v.* Do. (Dost) As in "Dus thee know?" –Do you know?

E

EARL STERNDALE. *Prop.n.* Locally known as *'Steender'*. The earliest references I can find for the village is *Stenredile* in 1244, *Sternedale* in 1251, *Erlisstenerdale* in1330, *Stener-a-dale* in 1415, *Sterndall* in 1531, Erlesterdale in1555, and *Earlesterdalle*. It is also given as Stryndall. (R.M.)

The area was held by William de Ferrars, Earl of Derby in1244.

EDITCH. *n.* (eddish, or hedditch) The corrupted rendering of the word *'Headage'*, or the secondary growth of grass which regenerates after the hay has been harvested. When the milking cattle are *'turned inter editch'* in the Autumn, their milk yield rises with the stimulus of fresh, young grass, - though not with quite the same dramatic results of Spring grass. (R.M., p.19, also W.P.F., p.117.)

ERN. *n.* The heron. E.g. " 'ast seed th'ern?" - Have you seen the heron?

ESS. *n.* Ashes from the fire. An *'Ess-hole'* was the squarish hole built below the level of the kitchen flagstones, just if front of the grate-front of the kitchen 'range'(see below). The 'ess-hole' was covered by a cast-iron grating with narrow slits in it. The ashes from the fire would be riddled through the bottom of the fire basket, with a poker, dropping onto the iron grating. The fine ashes would fall through the grating. Any large pieces would be thrown back onto the fire. The 'ess-hole'(also sometimes called an ash-pit) would be emptied, depending on its size, perhaps once or twice a month, and the fine, riddled 'ess' used for either mortar, or mixed with hair from horses, cattle or goats for plastering internal walls.

EYE-SERVER. *n.* A hired labourer who only labours when his employer is watching.

F

FAFFING. v. Fussy, ineffectual dithering. e.g. "Wot art' faffin' abairt at?"

FAGEL. n. (Soft 'g', as in "fadgel") – A heap of, or an excessive amount. E.g. "I saw 'im eatin' a greet fagel o' chips." Or, "only a bit, non a big fagel"- not a lot, please.

FAWCE. *adj.* (*Fause* or *force*) Describing someone's coercive or manipulative influence. (T.H., Vol.8, p.305).

In a child it would be used to describe their 'cute', winning persuasion. In an adult, this adjective would serve as a warning as to someone's possible trickery or two-facedness.

FETTLE. *v.* To exhaust, or tire out. The term might be used as: "That fettled 'im!"

Also *v.* *'In fine fettle'* – can mean to be in good condition.

FLITTING. v. Moving house. A common phrase being: "Friday flit, short sit" – Don't move house on a Friday, you'll not stay there long.

FLAGS. *n.* The square or oblong sandstone paving slabs put down as floors in houses and farm buildings, also used for pavements and yards.

FLEAKS. *n.* (pronounced Fleeks or Flayks) Hurdles. Movable pieces of fencing in lengths of around 5 or 6 feet , and between 3 to 4 feet high. Used as temporary enclosures at sheep sales, penning at routine husbandry, lambing time, shearing time, etc.

In olden times they would be made of horizontally interwoven hazel with stouter vertical pieces forming the frame, and with a protruding spiked peg at either end which could be trodden or hammered into the ground. Multiple *fleaks* were joined up to make multi-sized pens. Later they were made from light iron, rather like 'mini-gates' in inter-connecting permutations. Sometimes they would have solid sheeting of galvanised tin, plywood or even hard plastic.

Many a new gap in a dry-stone wall has been blocked up with a *fleak,* or any decrepit spare gate, when the farmer didn't have quite enough time to repair the wall. It was often a source of lively debate to see how long a time such a temporary defence against marauding sheep would be effective and then become rather too permanent. (R.M. p.21)

FLINKERING. *v.* Light snow drifting down without any breeze or wind. A charmingly onomatopoeic word that perfectly describes the event. (W.P.F., p.124.)

FRAB. *v.* Fidget or move in discomfort. Also to tease and make uncomfortable.

FRIDGE. *v.* To irritate, especially from clothing which is uncomfortable to sensitive skin. (T.H., Vol.6, p.255.)

FODDERGANG. n. (or *Fodderbing,* or *Fodderems.*) In later-built larger *shippons,* the long narrow pathway in front of the cattle (about a good yard wide) where hay, or any other foodstuffs, could be carried down and fed to the animals from the front.

FOLLOWERS. *n.* Any young cattle, or especially calves with their dams, i.e. not weaned, still suckling. (R.M. p.21)

FOW. *adj.* Ugly, unpleasant countenance. Especially associated with a virago, termagant or any other unattractive, disagreeable woman. E.g. "Er's a raight fow-faced un."

There is a local saying "As fow as Morridge woes!" - As ugly as the walls at Morridge, an area between Flash village, Quarnford and "The Royal Cottage" Inn on the Leek, Staffordshire road.

One story goes that one Winter many years ago, a man was walking in a blizzard from Leek to Buxton. The snow was very, very deep. Suddenly the man's leg shot down a hole. With great difficulty he extricated his leg from the hole, only to find it completely black. Then he realized he had put his foot down the chimney of "The Royal Cottage" Inn's chimney. Some blizzard!

FRIM. *adj.* 'Fresh' with new grass growth, especially in Spring.

That particular succulent green colour of vibrant, vigorous promise.

FULLOCK. *n.* Any surge of water after heavy rain. Also *v.* To drop down ungainly onto a chair or sofa in an exhausted state state. e.g. " 'Er fullocked dairn ont' th'settee."

42

G

GADDING. *v.* Excitedly going off to an occasion. On seeing someone smartly dressed, the question might be – "Wheer't thay gaddin' off to?" - Probably borrowed from the startled charging around of cattle, with their tails high in the air, especially in summertime, when *'worried'* and bitten by Gadflies. (*see below*)

GADFLIES. *n.* The larvae of these insects, being the troublesome 'warbles'. The life-cycle of the Gad or Warble-fly is both particularly interesting and hideous at the same time. The eggs are laid by the mature gadflies, along with severe biting, around the lower legs of cattle in the heat of summer. These eggs enter the bloodstream and migrate through their host's bodies over the next months to the area along the top of the back.

Here they pupate just under the hide, gradually boring through and hatch out in latish Spring. When these 'warbles' hatch out they fall onto the ground, fly, and mate as adult Gadflies, biting the legs of the cattle again to complete the cycle, thus they live for the vast majority of their lives inside a cow. (What a way to run your life!)

Severe infestation ruins the hides for leather usage. It is often said Gadflies will not cross rivers. Application of Organo-phosphorous treatment has virtually eliminated 'Warbles'. But it has had a very contentious and deleterious effect on the health of farmers who were obliged by Government legislation to administer these highly toxic chemicals. Certainly not enough warning was given initially to farmers as to the possible long term effects of using such poisonous compounds. In field conditions when applying such treatments it is virtually impossible to eliminate accidental contamination of human skin.

The comfort of the cattle was the obvious and desired advantage. The financial comfort of the Chemical Companies and the Ministry of Agriculture officers was also apparent. The Farmer's pocket was hit twice: once with the cost of buying and administering the treatments, and secondly helping to lower the price of hide through a glut of good and less 'imperfect' hides on the market. Such is life!

GALLIVANTING. v. – Going on a day out, or attending an unnecessarily diversionary occasion, - usually when things that needed to be done were left undone. "Wheer art thee gallivantin' off to?"

GANDER. v. To look at. *'Gandering'* - looking at intently. Perhaps coming from the stretched-out neck of an inquisitive male goose?

GANSEY. n. A jumper, cardigan or even *any* outer garment worn over the shirt.

GAPPING. v. (or *Gap-walling.*) Mending broken-down walls, especially in Spring, after the ravages of Wintertime, or the bloody-minded vandalisation by escaping sheep.

GARGLE. n. (or *Garget*) Mastitis in dairy cattle. Inflammation of the udder caused by bacteria entering through the teat canals, resulting in swelling and associated with thick clots and occasionally blood in the milk.

GIMPY. *adj.* Lame.

GINNEL. (Gennel.) n. a narrow pathway running between the walled backyards of houses.

GILT. A young female pig, - a maiden sow.

GLOPPENED *adv.* (*Gloppent*) Lost for words, dumbstruck. "'Ay wur raight gloppent!" - "He couldn't speak!"

GODFATHER. n. A cheap and temporary repair on any door. Splicing-in or tacking-to some rough piece of timber to prolong the door's life. An economic necessity that usually stuck out like a 'sore thumb', and annoyed the 'out-of-work' joiner!

GOMEREL; n. A foolish person, (C.P. p.11)

44

GONDER. *n.* A male goose. (A gander.) Not really a different word, just an example of the almost perverse way that dialect has of almost wantonly pronouncing words differently at most occasions!

It may be, arguably, that people use these 'regionalities' as a kind of clannish defence mechanism against 'outsiders' or, conversely, used as a mode of 'belonging' to a certain geographical region. It may just be that the vowels and consonants used in any dialect is then the result of this static historical anchorage in the birthplace, and therefore little or no desire to alter sounds expediently.

GORMERS. *n.* The upright, 'gate-like' structures fixed at either end of a hay-cart, or four-wheeled-dray, which are designed to keep the loaded hay contained. Two diagonal arms on either side of each 'gate' fix the gormers in an upright or slightly outwardly-sloped position to the main flat body of the hay-cart. (R.M. p.23)

GORMLESS. *adj.* (also *Gormin' at*) Stupid, no idea or incentive. Also, looking at, perplexed, in a stupefied manner. "Worrart thee gormin' at?" – "What are you looking stupidly at?"

GOSTER. v. To look or stare at uncomprehendingly. Not necessarily as a simple minded person, more someone who couldn't quite work it out yet, or as having not quite "twigged" the situation. This word has a slightly different nuance than *gormless,* and describes someone's perplexity at, say, possibly having had the wind taken out of their sails rather than being dim-witted. (S.P., p.28.)

GRADELY. *adj.* Worthy, well-fashioned, deserving praise or respect. (C.P. *p.2)*

GRAUNCH. v. Grinding the teeth. Also incompetent changing of gears in a car, or on a tractor, by bad clutching or rough gear stick operation.

GRESS. *n.* Grass. Also *Gress dey* – The 'official' day that the cattle are 'turned-out' in Springtime with enough grass to support them. Usually unofficially marked as the 18th of May in this part of Derbyshire, when stock have enough pasture to support them without excessive supplementary feed..

GLOOMING. *v.* Hot, dull, humid weather with full cloud cover, thundery and also described as 'close'(see above). The expression would be – "It's gloomin' fer heat." - i.e. more of the same.

GROOP. (Group) *n.* The dung channel. (W.P.F., p.125.) In old-fashioned *shippons* (cow-sheds) the *groop* was the stone-slabbed, (later concrete) lower area in between the cow's tied-up standing/lying area (or *boose* – see above) and the clean pathway, for the cowman to walk and where the churns and milking units stood. This was, of course, long before the milking parlours and zealous sanitary regulations of the present times.

GUMTION. *n.* Probably can be also spelt '*Gumption*', but is pronounced hereabouts without the plosive 'p' - (i.e. 'gumshon') . (T.H., Vol.6, p.255.)

H

HACKING. *v.* After mowing a field of grass for haymaking, this was the practice of cutting the last couple of feet of still-standing grass right beside the wall or hedge which the horse-drawn mowing machine couldn't quite get at. Usually done by hand with a scythe, and in order to thriftily get the very last little bit of fodder possible. It was also a way of not blunting, or breaking, knives on the mowing machine by the odd stone that had fallen off the wall and not been noticed.

This rather tight-fisted and over-zealous chore died out in the 1950s and 1960s with the advent of larger and more expensive machinery. It was considered more prudent to leave a wider swath of uncut grass near the wall than risk monetary and time wastage with breakdowns.

With the advent of silage making, and also the difficulty of drying overgrown and damp grass under walls and hedges, the more relaxed attitude of turning livestock into the field to do the 'Hacking' (or *'Badging'* as it was also called) after the crop had been harvested seemed a more sensible approach. Grandfathers would have frowned, but hopefully not commented.

(Also) HACKING. *n.* Another dish from that most versatile animal, the pig. Take the liver and boil it well until it falls apart. Render the liefs of fat, saved separately, into lard, and from the 'scratchings' left over mix with the boiled liver into a rough-textured paste, adding seasoning. Press the mixed paste into basins and allow to cool and set naturally. To serve, simply upturn the basin over a plate, knock out the 'hacking' and carve into slices. Eat cold, especially with guests that have stayed far too long a while.

Other treats from the pork butcher are black puddings, savoury ducks, hazlett, etc, etc, but why go on? Too many counties claim them as their own inventions.

Save the animal, - eat a vegetarian!

HAMES. *n.* The pair of shaped iron, or brass, pieces of draught-harness that fitted either side of the horse's collar, to which were attached the trace chains of the shafts of whatever cart or implement was being pulled..

HANTLE. *n.* A handful. (S.P., p.29.)

HAYCOCK. *n.* Temporary small mounds of hay left in the field to dry out. Sometimes covered with small canvas or tarpaulin sheets if the weather was inclement for a while.. The term was 'fielding' the hay. (W.P.F., p.125.)

HAY-KNIFE. *n.* A broad, deep-bladed tool with its handle set cross-wise, used for cutting out 'sets' or 'cesses' of hay into an armful to be carried from the haystack to the stalled cattle.

HIRING FAIR. *n.* Usually held on New Year's Day. Farm labourers and young lads looking for work would assemble on the village green, and be 'taken on' or hired for a full years work.

I'll hand over here to my paternal Grandfather's personal experience for a few paragraphs.

It is the late 1890s. My Grandfather, who ran away from home at twelve years of age, went to Longnor Hiring Fair and 'took on' as a hired farm worker for £5 a year, plus a new 'working top-coat'.

Towards the end of the year's contract, unscrupulous farmers would give their labourers unreasonable or excessive outdoor work in the fields trying to make them fed up and therefore quit the job. If you left before the exact year was completed your wages, in total, were forfeited. You were paid once at the end of the contracted year. The binding element was spitting on your own hand and shaking that of your employer, and accepting a shilling – the 'hiring shilling'. Workers often 'lived-in' with the farmer, in an attic bedroom, or over the stable, with a small fireplace. Food was provided, plain, but enough. My Grandfather stuck it out, and was paid.

He went to the next hiring fair and 'took on' again with the same employer for £7 a year, again, plus a new working coat. And a third term at £9 a year.

My father started work for my Grandfather in 1935, (leaving school at 14 years old), for two shillings and sixpence a fortnight, or £6 a year. That quickly rose to £1 per week when he was 18.

I started working for my father in 1966, at 16 years old, for £4 a week, - £208 a year. True, you lived at home free of charge, with hardly any expenses, When I had saved up £1000 in my bank account after 5 years hard work, I thought I had done well. How times change, yet it's only just over 40 years ago. Not that long really.

HOGG. *n.* A sheep around 12 months old. Really, in between a lamb and a mature sheep, but not exactly definable in precise months, but certainly right up to the first shearing, and even that dependant on the animal being kept for either breeding or slaughter. Sorry to be imprecise, but any farmer knows what I mean! (See Mouthing-Forward below)

HOLLIN. *n.* Holly, the evergreen tree. As in the place names: Hollin's Barn, Hollin Knowle and Hollinsclough. (J.B., 1997.)

HOPPLES *n.* (or Hobbles). An appliance used on sheep. The practise of tying a front and a back leg together of any wayward, trespassing sheep! Often this is the amorous ram. - (or 'tup' being the usual local description.)

One obvious reason for this restrictive practice being: not so much as the neighbour annoyed at your animal's free grazing on his land, but more as a precaution against lambs being born earlier than desired. Strips of strong material, even leather, are tied round the fetlocks, (heels or ankles), linking two legs together. The 'natural' gait of the animal is confused for a while, thus slowing its movements and wall-climbing propensities! Eventually, sheep being what they are, that of a singularly resourceful character, they 'learn' first to walk with the appliance, then run and finally escape again. The hopple is then switched to link opposite front and back legs, or side to side, etc. After all the permutations have been exhausted, without success, the farmer usually admits defeat, and either telephones the Auctioneer, or shows the offending animal a particularly vibrant patch of mint in the garden! (see also *Sheep-couples.*)

HORN. *v.* To put up with. "A'l 'orn it!" – "I'll put up with it!" or, "Tha's made a bull, tha mun 'orn it!" - "You've made a blunder; you'll have to stick with it!" Also, to force- feed liquid medicines into a sick animal by using the old-fashioned 'drenching-horn'. This was a sawn-off cow's horn with the central pith removed. Held upright in the hand, the liquid drench was poured into the horn. By 'nosing' (see below) the animal with the left hand, the medicine could be tipped from the drenching-horn down the throat of the animal. It sounds easy, it isn't! The drenching-horn usually had a loop of strong tape fixed through the narrow, solid point of the 'horn' to hang it up by, I still have the one that Mr. Frank Bagnall gave to me. It was made from the horn of an Ayrshire cow. (See *Ayrsh'orn lip* above) Also, if someone was eating greedily or quickly, it could be said that they were: "'ornin' it inter 'imsen." i.e. 'getting it down his neck!'

HORSE BRASSES. *n.* The harness used for 'gearing–up' a horse to any cart or implement was made of thick, hand-stitched leather with brass buckles. Gradually, over the centuries, especially in the 19th and early 20th, more and more ornamental pieces of brass were sewn onto the harness. Show harness was the ultimate epitome of this art form, usually only seen nowadays as an advertising feature for breweries 'turn-outs', hung around the beams of pubs or festooning die-hard farmhouses. Newly-polished horse brasses are an eye-rewarding sight, especially to those who don't have to polish them.

One cynic once remarked that even when the farmer had done his day's work, he then liked to sit and look at it at night. All the same, it is a marvellous sight to see a shire-horse in full show harness, they always get a round of applause at agricultural events. Whether it's an appreciation of the spectacle, or a conscience-pricked thankfulness we don't have to work like that any more, I'm not sure.

HORSE MILL *n.* A small mill driven by a horse walking in a circle. (R.M. p.26) see also *JINNY RING* below.

HOWAT. Or more properly, "How art?" -. How are you? The reply could be "non bad" – quite well, "fair ter middlin'" – very well, or "am o raight, owathey?" – I'm in tip-top form, what about yourself?

HUCKREL. n. A young, slovenly female, - human! Especially one who is perhaps if not of doubtful morals then certainly of questionable virtue. (Strange how rather priggish and sanctimonious this seems nowadays.)

HUMMERING. *v.* The very particular sound sheep make in the hour or so just before they give birth, and really at no other time in the year. When you're 'sitting up at night' with them, and doing the regular 'rounds of the lambing-shed', you move quietly, or just stand, watch and listen. This special sound, a cross between a gentle nasal 'snortling' and a back-of-the-throat 'enclosed bleating' is a sure sign of imminent parturition. It is a very definitive sound that you become used to over years of experience. It is an exciting, anxious, and really is quite a beautiful, almost humbling sound. 'Hummering' is the best and only human way of expressing it phonetically.

To digress a little, no matter how many hundreds of times I have assisted at birthings, whether cattle, sheep, or occasionally pigs, new life never loses its thrill or wonder.

Farmers might be accused by some less-enlightened people as being somewhat 'financial' in their treatment of their animals. I can only say I would often say "welcome" under my breath after a successful delivery, and always felt wretched at those times when things didn't go right. Yes, we keep animals to live, breed, thrive and be marketed for our own livelihood, but that doesn't mean we farm without kindness, or awareness of our stocks needs, comfort and veterinary treatment when needed. Animals can't tell you they're feeling ill, so there is no substitute for that old-fashioned word 'stockmanship'.

When the time comes to either sell or dispatch an animal it should always be done with pride, compassion, appreciation and above all, respect. Animals will always thrive and respond well in the custodianship of a diligent, caring and conscientious farmer.

HUTCH-UP. *v.* Draw up to. - Especially the fireplace. As a question, or command, Asking others to make room for another. "Cum thee in, mek room, hutch up t'th'fire."

I

IDLEBACK. *n.* Blocks of fire-hardened clay left over from the pottery kilns of North Staffordshire. These greyish lumps, often referred to as fired 'sagger marl' were then dipped in a bucket of water and rubbed against smooth masonry. It was used, for example, to 'whiten' the stone window sills or door jambs in a decorative manner. Had a similar effect to '*Donkey stone.*' (see above.)

IN-CALF. *adj.* The pregnant state of cattle. An odd description, as it is always said: "That cow's in-calf.", yet, literally, it is the calf that is *in* the cow. Thus it follows; *in-lamb, in-foal, in-pig,* etc. ('*in-kittle*' is the expression for a pregnant cat).

J

JACK. What springs to mind is 'calling-up' pigs to the trough, and would be "Jack, jack, jack, jack, jack" shouted quickly over and over. I've also heard people shout "Boff, Boff, Boff, Boff." Either sound doesn't have to be uttered for very long; pigs being very appreciative feeders. They would even probably come to the trough even if you shouted "Critical Theory!", "Existentialism!" or "George Orwell!", though "Sausages!" might seem a shade reprehensible.

It must be pointed out that given the right conditions and management, pigs are the cleanest of farm animals.

JED. *adv.* Dead. e.g. "Eyts jed!" – "It's dead!"

JINKY-BACKED. *adj.* Crooked-backed. (see also 'Charley' on 'is back'.

JINNY-RING. *n.* In the yard at my family's farm, "Glutton Grange", there was a circular paved track around a central pole. This assemblage was joined by various metal gears and shafts to a straw-chopping machine in the loft of the stable. It could also operate a turnip-pulper. The horse, or donkey, was harnessed to the arm-pole fixed to the central pole outside and walked slowly round in a circle. The series of shafts, gears and canvas belts drove the mechanisms inside the building. (*Horse-millne*, R.M. p.26, also W.P.F., p.125.)

JONNOCK. *adv.* Honourable, true, steadfast, loyal. " 'Ees jonnock!" – He's a good friend.

JUMPER. *n.* A quick repair to a fallen piece of dry-stone wall. Whether it meant 'jumped the wall back up' or, if left, might be a tantalizing place for sheep to start jumping over?

K

KETCH-OWD. A composite word of 'catch and hold'. i.e. "give a hand!" A stern command to those who were unwilling to help, or idly 'standing back'"

KICKING-STRAP. *n.* A stout leather strap with a fixed central loop. Used to restrain a nervous, newly-calved heifer or an ill-tempered cow at milking time.
It is first put around one rear leg, just above the hock, passing the 'tail end of the strap through the central loop, passed back around the other leg, and fastened tightly to the buckle end to form a 'figure-of-eight' around both legs. Used as a very last resort when all patience has been exhausted. Any milking cow thus restrained never comes to its full potential of production. The use of such a tool is an admission of failure to sufficiently calm the cow….and would be better applied to the cowman.

KIGGLY. *adj.* Uneven, unstable or wobbly.

KINDLING. *n.* Pronounced as 'k-INN-dling', not as in 'being kind'. Firewood, especially, small chopped sticks, or off-cuts of sawn timber, used to start the fire in the hearth place. Firewood generally. (W.P.F., p.118.)

KINDLE. *v.* – To bear young, (especially cats).
The phrase would be, on seeing the cat was pregnant, "Ay up, th'kyats i'kindle." (either *in kindle*, or *in kittle*) . (W.P.F., p.118.) There was also sometimes said a short phrase concerning young couples who were falling out, or shouting and crying at each other - "Faightin' 'n scraightin' orlis gyets kyat i' kittle!" – (Fighting and crying always gets the cat pregnant) The allusion to caterwauling felines, either amorous or unresponsive, on the rooftops is metaphorically apt!

KIVVER. *n.* A group of sheaves, or stooks, of corn. Usually ten, (some claim twelve), sheaves to a kiver. 'Stooking' corn was done thus; working in a team of two people, 1. firstly, two sheaves were carried, then stood upright together by the first person, 2. The second person would carry two more sheaves to this point, placed them oppositely against the first two, making a 'four-square'. 3. The first person was meanwhile carrying in two more sheaves and placed them at opposite sides of the kiver. Then as the second person carried in two more and placed those sheaves on the 'free' sides, making eight, - i.e. four in the inner square, four on the outer square. The first person then placed two sheaves on top of and over the eight, as a double small sloping 'roof', in case of rain. Just as the second person tied two bands of twine over and round the kiver to secure it altogether. The carting to the barn came later.

KRATCH. *n.* (cratch) In older cowsheds, the fixed wooden-slatted angled racks at the cattle's head height. Hay would be dropped into the kratches from the hay-loft, over and above, or carried down the *fodderbings* (see above) and fed from the front.   *Field-cratches* were early wooden, (later metal, with wheels, movable feeding frames for either sheep or 'out-wintered' cattle.

L

LAMBING STORMS. *n.* Light flurries of snow at the beginning of Spring, coinciding with lambing time. Not serious storms, but enough to say that winter hasn't quite finished.

LAP. *n.* A measure of hay from a bale. Approximately 10 – 12 'laps' to an average bale.

LAUNDINGS. *n.* (*Landings*) Guttering on a roof, either wooden or metal, (see *Lander*, Rt. Hon. L.D. 1862 – 3, Vol.3, p.116).

LARROP. *v.* To swallow your meal quickly. *"Larrop it dairn thi!"* - "Get it down!"

(Also) LARROPING. *v.* Moving giddishly, in an ineffectual, ridiculous manner. "'E wur larropin' up an dairn th'place." – he was running up and down, getting nowhere.

LATCH-LIFTING. *v.* Literally, lifting someone's door latch. Going to visit neighbours unannounced. Always a pleasant divergence from the daily round of work and bed. A chance to catch up on, or further the news. – A chance to go gossiping really. In those faraway days doors were rarely locked and people were all too pleased to 'neighbour' and talk of life.

LECKIN'CAN. *n.* A watering can

LEET. *n.* A light. "Ast gerra leet?" Have you got a light?

LESH. *adv.* Smooth, polished. Just like a stone, or concrete, feeding-trough. "Tha'rt as lesh as a pig-truff!" – " You're as smooth as a pig-trough!" An endearing (?) comment on someone's complexion. Never fails to impress the girls. A chat-up line second to none.

LIG. – Lie idly , a sluggardly or slovenly approach to the day. "Tha'll lig i'bed o'dee!" – "You'll lie in bed all day!"

LUKIN' *v.* (Looking, or seeing, to it.) As in preparing, or getting ready generally, a meal. "Er's lukin' tea." – She's getting the tea-time meal ready.

LUMMOCK. *n.* A large, ungainly person. (W.P.F., p.125.)

LUMPY-TUMS. *n.* (Lumpitums.) A little water and milk heated in equal measure, with a handful of oatmeal added and stirred to the personally-preferred consistency. Not quite the same as porridge, though similar. Often taken by children at supper-time (J.B., 1997).

M

MACON. *n.* A cross between mutton and bacon. It is actually made from sheep meat, but is salted down and later fried, just as bacon would be. Definitely different. A term from the 'war years'.

MADE-UP. *adj.* Full of a cold, or flu. e.g."Made-up wi' a cowd."

MARD. *adj.* Spoilt, petulant, childish. E.g. "'Ees a raight mard." (he really is spoiled) Also, 'mardarse' (coarse, - a brat.)

MARTIN. *n.* A bovine that is naturally barren from birth. In same-sex twins in cattle, usually both will breed. In mixed-sex twins, usually, but not always, it is the female which will not breed. Certainly a far higher percentage of females from mixed twins are prone to be *martins*.

Twin-breeding cattle usually pass that particular gene onto their offspring. I personally never liked twin calves – you often get two small calves, which are difficult to rear successfully, and the dam is often poor in 'condition' because of the debilitating drain on her resources of carrying twins, so much so that the milk yield for that lactation is often lower than hoped for. Extra feeding of the dam, when twins are known of, isn't really an option, in that the two calves are

58

grown to normal size, resulting in possible calving difficulties. I have heard the term *'Castlemartin'* also, but I know not if it is the same.

At 'Glutton Grange', my father once had a cow that produced 14 calves in 7 years. It started with a single calf, followed by five sets of twins and finished with triplets. We never reared a live calf, and her lactations were well below average.

MAYBLOBS. *n.* Marsh-marigolds. Kingcups.

MIDDEN. *n.* A dung-heap, sometimes partly surrounded by a wall, or adjacent to a farm building, but not always. They could be just piled up in the field.

MILKING STOOL. *n.* The three-legged, (for stability) flat-topped stool, usually made from elm or oak, used by men and women to sit on at the side of the cow at milking time.

For his seventh birthday present, my father, Frank Edward Holland, was given a milking stool! Every morning he had to milk four 'drying-off' cows. With his three elder brothers, (Donald, b.1917, Albert b.1918, Herbert b.1919) my father then helped my Grandfather to deliver milk around Harpur Hill village before going to school.

MITHER. *v.* Worry, pressure. "Yer mitherin' mey nair!" – "you're pressuring me now!" or, "Am mithered deeth!" - "I'm worried to death!"

MIZZLED. *v.* – Gone missing. e.g. "'E's mizzled off sumweer," – He's gone missing somewhere.

MOOCHING. *v.* Moving slowly, indolently, with little purpose. (Also – Spying on courting couples!)

MOUTHING-FORWARD *v.* A term used about a pen of youngish, breeding sheep. To explain;

1. Firstly, (for non-farmers), sheep only have teeth on their bottom jaw, - the upper jaw is used as a hard 'pad' to bite against whilst grazing.

2.Generally; lambs have 8 'milk-teeth' up to nearly one year old. They then get 2 large, mature, secondary teeth which displace the 2 milk-teeth in the middle of the jaw.

3. The next year they produce two further mature teeth either side the first two mature ones. At this stage they have usually been shorn once and will be known as a 'Theave' (or Gimmer) if kept as a breeding female, - a 'Wether' (or Hogg) if a castrated male going for slaughter, though sometimes these are not shorn, - and a Shearling (or Sharling) if kept as a breeding entire male. - Are you still with me?

4. The following year the sheep will push up 2 more mature teeth on either side of the four it already has, thus making 6 mature and 2 remaining milk-teeth on the outside. The terms used then are ; 'Double-Theave' for a breeding female, - (the castrated males have usually been butchered by now,) - and a 'Two-Shear' as a breeding male, (is there any need to point out that he has now been shorn twice?)

5. The following year the animal will displace the remaining two milk teeth at the extreme sides of the 6 mature teeth, now making 8 mature teeth. The female is finally known now as a 'Ewe', (or full-mouthed.) The breeding male now becomes a 'Ram' or 'Tup'. Well done, if you're still reading!

6. With age the mature teeth start to either wear down to little stumps or become long and loose, eventually dropping out. – (Hence the term "A bit long in the tooth!") The term used then is 'broken-mouthed'.

7. To go back to 'mouthing-forward', (which seems an awful long time ago,) any of these permutations of teeth and age are not set in tablets of stone. They are a good general guide as to the general age of a pen of animals for sale. Whilst the farmer gives a truthful description as to the age of his batch of sheep, he may add the codicil term – "one or two mouthing-forward." It is a respectable admission of their dental state, not a means of misrepresentation of their age and therefore possible future productive life.

8. Cattle have the same 'teeth-with-age' patterns as sheep, - but enough already!

MOWDYWORP. *n.* (Mouldywarp) The mole. "Th' mowdy-worps'r pushin' up!" – The moles are active. (*esp. Springtime.*)

MOWLY. *adj.* Mouldy. (Pronounced 'm-owl-y – as in 'owl'.)

MUCHER. *n.* A negatively-used label for a dim-witted or lazy individual, "E's non a mucher." i.e. - he isn't much good, or hasn't much going for him.

MUTNA, *v.* (MUNNA) *v.* Must not. - e.g. "Aaay, tha munna do that!"

N

NESH. *adj.* Not used to raw, outdoor existence. A mild insult to a "hot-house plant" person would be to say; "Th'art nesh!" Also a term used to describe hay that is not quite ready to either cart in, or bale, i.e. needs more time left out in the sun to 'crisp' up, or to dry out. 'Nesh' hay will heat up in the barn, or loft, and could cause a natural 'combustion' fire. (Rt. Hon L.D., 1863 – 4, Vol.2, p.14.)

NOOK-SHOTTEN. *adj. and v.* A crack in the gable-end of a house around the chimney -stack. –Usually caused through the expansion and contraction of the stonework around the flue. A cracked inglenook.

NOSING. *v.* If a set of *barnacles* (see above) were not available, then a fractious, nervous or belligerent animal could be restrained in this way: With the animal's head held tightly underneath the handler's left arm and side, temporarily obliterating the animal's vision, and the handler's right hand thumb and fingers grippingly tightly the animal's septum. (see also *'tailing'*)

NOUS. *n.* Common-sense or reasoning. Also someone said to have '*no nous*' would be deemed to lack initiative or drive. (T.H., Vol. 6, p.255.)

NURDLING. *v.* The sound that babies make when gently grumbling. Not as when in painful gripes, but that slightly uncomfortable, fractious, guttural whingeing just prior to a full-blown howl.

O

O'ERTHROWN. *adj.* Describing a sheep that has rolled onto it's back and cannot right itself. This may happen at almost any time of the year, but mainly when they are over-fat or just prior to shearing time when the fleece is at it's bulkiest. In such a position the animal begins to bloat, exacerbating the problem. Needless to say, if un-noticed for a couple of days the animal will die.

OH-HOAG. The call to sheep to follow the shepherd, with his faithful dog making sure that all do so. (Or, more likely, a call used to entice sheep to come to the troughs to be fed.) An evocative sound that still echoes and re-echoes round the hills today.

I feel certain it is a call continually used by shepherds since the biblical Abel first started sheep-farming, (Genesis, Ch.IV, v.2.). Adam was of course a gardener (Genesis Ch.II, v.15) and Cain an arable farmer, (Genesis, Ch.IV, v.2.) That was in the good old days when The Ministry of Agriculture had only one officer – God.

This plaintive call is usually delivered as "Oh-hooooag, oh-hooooag!" with the stress on the long second syllable. The 'oag' part of it is sounded like the 'oag' in ogre. A slight variation can be "Yaaaah-hoag, Yaaaaah-hoag!", stressing and elongating the first syllable. – surprisingly, sheep can understand both. Who said they weren't intelligent?

ORLIS. – (Allus.) – Always. "Av orlis toed thee!" I've always told you!"

ORTS. *n.* The dross from the mangers collected up and usually given to the "dry" pregnant cows, or non-milk producing cattle, or often the bull! Literally, the 'sweepings-up'.

OTIL. *n.* A finger-stall. A strong covering of canvas, or leather, to shield a bandaged digit. With two tapes or strings attached, thus tied around the wrist to keep it in place.

OVERLAIN. *v.* Over slept. Not woken up at the desired time. (W.P.F., p.120.)

OWAT. – (or Owart?) - How are you, mate? - "Owat surrey?"

P

PANCHEON. n. A large circular earthenware vessel, which is internally glazed, but not on the outside. Roughly 12 inches high, 18 inches in circumference at the top, and having narrowing sides going down to a relatively small base of about 6 inches. Used to 'set up' milk so that the cream rises to the broadest surface at the top of the vessel. The cream could then be skimmed off more easily for butter-making. The vessel could also be used for curds in cheese-making, or preserving eggs under isinglass, pickling onions or really any storage in general. Principally a dairy utensil.

PETTY. n. (Privy.) - Lavatory. An outside "dry-bucket" closet. Often the seat was one wide plank with two holes cut into it side by side, i.e. adult and child size. There is even a wonderful example of a 'three-seater' at Harley Grange. Petties usually had a bolt on the inside for some privacy, but rarely had a lock on the outside - unlikely to have contents stolen.

PICKEL. n. Another word for a *Pitchfork* (see below.) (J.B., 1997.)

PIGEON-PIE. n. There used to be a practise of waiting until a pair of woodpigeons had hatched their chicks. After about a week, lads would climb up the tree and tie the young 'squabs' by one leg only, with soft string, through the bottom of the nest. After the parents had fed the squabs for around six to eight weeks, i.e. just before they would be about to fly the nest, it was a simple job to climb the tree again and bring down the fattened squabs for the pot. By tying one leg only, the young could move enough, but with out getting tangled up. Pigeon-pie was a delicacy, and this way was cheaper than a shotgun and cartridges.

PINCHED. *adj.* Describing stock that are short of pasture. "theer pinched fer gress."

PICKING-HOLE. *n.* (Pitching-hole.) - A small doorway, usually about a yard square, through which hay (loose or baled) was *pitch-forked* through from the cart into the barn or hayloft. Usually square, though occasionally circular on more sheltered farms where cereals might be grown. Though more the case in the south of the county really.

PITCHFORK. *n.* A two-pronged spring-steel fork used for loading loose hay onto carts, with various lengths of wooden shafts to suit the height of the man using it. The prongs average about 9 inches to a foot long, roughly 6 to 9 inches apart, joined onto a y-shaped piece that has a central haft for the wooden shaft. A *Bale-fork* had much narrower prongs and was a later development.

POBS. *n.* A mugful of milk heated then thickened with small pieces of bread, plus a little seasoning. A bedtime food/drink eaten with a teaspoon by the elderly, children or infirm.

POLEAXE. *n.* Wooden-hafted iron tool used for slaughtering stock. In size like a small pickaxe, with a point at one end and a thicker hollowed-out tube at the other. The latter end used to 'drill' a hole out of the front of the skull, before insertion of a thin flexible steel wire to pierce the brain and spinal column. Occasionally they had a short blade at one end.

POOSE. *n.* Rubbishy article. Poor stock. Unworthy characteristics. 'Bad doers.'

PUDDING-PIE. *n.* An ancient small, field lime-kiln. Mainly for local agricultural usage. Round in shape, resembling an upturned pudding dish, hence the nick-name. Rather like a large igloo or beehive.

PUTHERING. *v.* Describing smoke 'down-draughting' into a room in windy weather. Or describing a heavy snow-fall in very windy, blizzard conditions. (W.P.F., p.120. also J.B., 1997.)

Q

QUEEDLE. *v.* A see-saw. Similar meaning to *Queegle* below

QUEEGLE. *v.* To rock back and forth. (see *Crow-queggler* above)

QUILE. *n.* (also pronounced Quoil, Coil.) Usually small heaps of hay gathered into lines ready to be loaded onto the hay-cart. Or small heaps of manure that have been dropped out of the horse-drawn muck-cart in lines at regular intervals around the fields in early Spring. These would be spread around by muck-forks later. It was said if you had three 'forkfuls' in the air at once, viz; one going up, one hanging in mid-air, and one coming down, then you were a good man at muckspreading!

QUP. (coo-up.) Calling cattle in for milking or to check on their well-being. The phrase is usually shouted – "Qup, qup, qup, cum-aaaaarn." Probably came from "cow come up, come on." – A variant is "O-co, O-co!" with the stress on the O. When entering a cowshed at night-time the words "Soooo, sooo, so-then." would be quietly uttered, for example when checking on a calving or ill animal, or to calm down an agitated one.

R

RACKS. *n.* Frames, either wooden or metal, for holding fodder for livestock. Either fixed to walls of buildings or moveable, whether free-standing or on wheels. .

RADDLE. *n.* Thick, oily paint applied to the chest and belly area of rams at 'tuppin' time' (late Autumn) to mark which ewes have been impregnated. The colour of the 'raddle' was changed and recorded over 21 day cycles to determine the batches of ewes mated in that period, and therefore an aid in management at predicted lambing time. The extra feeding of supplementary diet in late pregnancy and projected birthing times could be thus better managed. Also to ascertain and differentiate between the quality of various sires progeny. The modern equivalent being a sire-sign chest harness with waterproof colourants in a marker brickette. A promiscuous man could be justifiably admonished with the label of, "Ee wants raddlin' " to either deter him, or determine his conquests.

RAGGLE-POLE. *n.* A coarse word, describing the short, stout, rounded piece of wood fixed diagonally across a dark corner of a small farm building. Positioned about 2 feet off the floor, and in front of the necessary bucket-utensil right in the corner, it served as a crude lavatory seat. Sometimes there would be merely a backward-projecting sloped flagstone built through the wall of the building to an outside 'midden.' Usually used only by farm-hands or seasonal itinerant workers.

N.B. This was from the time of a much older generation who made the 'sarvent-mon' use a separate lavatory from the family, and even to sit at a separate table in the farmhouse kitchen to take their meals. Politically correct? - try starving. No 'benefits' in those days.

RAMMEL. *n.* – Rubbish, or worthless goods. "A load o' rammel!" (W.P.F., p.125.)

RAPSCALLION. *n.* A rogue, mischief-maker, or devious person.

RATCHEL. *n.* – Thin-soiled land over gravelly scree slopes, e.g. the top end of Hartington Dale.

RAUNGE. *v.* (rawnge or rawm)– Over-zealous action or excessive movement in general. This could appertain to someone over-emphasising the task in its operation, clumsily charging around and about the job in hand. Also, (coarsely), the excited mounting of cattle 'in bulling' i.e. on heat. Literally over-reaching. (see S.P., p.58.)

RID. *v.* To clear away snow from a road or path.(W.P.F., p.122.)

RIDDLE. *n.* A sieve (R.M. p.40, also S.P., p.58.))

RIGG. *n.* Any supposedly castrated male animal that had not been completely neutered successfully. Mistakes like that can occasionally happen. It was very annoying to find that some females had fallen pregnant to a male animal that was considered not of good enough constitution to breed from, i.e. one that had been castrated incorrectly and erroneously believed to be incapable of siring offspring.

RINDLE. *n.* Any small stream that runs continuously, not just in times of heavy rain. It is less than a brook or river. The rindle that surfaces and flows from Dowall Hall, past The Stannery and into the River Dove is a prime example.

RISSOM. *n.* The least amount or smallest particle. "They 'aven't a rissom of hay int' kratch!" – i.e. uncared for. (S.P., p.59.)

RODNEYING. v. Going on an unsolicited day off work, or hiding and idling about surreptitiously, or even going on a alcoholic drinking bender.

RODSTAKE. *n.* The piece of either wood or metal rod fixed vertically either side of the *'Boskin'* (see above) The Rodstake varies in length depending on the size of cattle being stalled, but usually between 2 and 3 feet. It enables the cow-chain, held by a running loop, to move freely up and down, depending on whether the animal was standing or lying down.

RONK. *adj.* Overgrown grass, difficult to mow and dry for hay. Also, (coarse slang), the over-active display of animals 'in heat'. Has been described of a few humans also.

ROPS. *n.* Intestines (etymological: ropes.) - (W.P.F., p.120.)

RUCK. *n.* A heap, or an amount of almost anything, - stones, sticks, sacks, sheep. folk.

RUCKSIONS. *n.* Commotions, trouble. E.g. – "Th'll be rucksions when thi Feyther gets wom!" – There'll be trouble when your dad gets home!"

RUM. *adj.* A few meanings. Anything from odd or different, to unworthy or distrustful. It can be either comically complimentary or caustically cautionary depending on the smile or frown on the speaker's face! - "Ee's a rum un!" could be taken many ways, the intonation or facial expression would be the best way to interpret the phrase.

S

SALTINGSTONE. *n.* Similar to a thrall (see below). Sandstone slabs horizontally arranged around cellars for 'salting' and storing meat as a means of preservation for the long, bleak Derbyshire winters. Also *'Salting Trough'-* A shallow sandstone trough for the initial process.

SAM-UP. *v.* To tidy up or clear away, especially the table after mealtimes. Also tools after finishing a job. (Rt.Hon. L.D., 1863 – 4, Vol.2.)

SEED. *v.* Saw, past tense of see. "A seed 'im" – I saw him.

SCOPE. *n.* A measuring, feeding utensil. Similar to a scoop, with a handle at one side, or end, to grasp it by, a saucer-like light metal pan with a handle. The word would be used in a phrase like: "That cow only wants half a scope o' corn - she's a bit sick."

SCOTCH HANDS. *n.* A pair of wooden butter pats. Used for making the newly-made farmhouse butter into the oblong shapes roughly 6" long, 3" deep and 3" wide, usually slightly proud of half a pound in weight. The rhythm of using a pair of scotch hands is a very particular thing to each person. My mother's method was as follows:

1. Two short quick pats to the top of the mound of fresh butter, already weighed out.

2. One simultaneous, sideways pat from both sides to begin forming a generally oblong shape, and, whilst still 'trapping' the butter, turning it through one 90 degree 'side' of the rough oblong.

3. Another sideways 'trapping' motion, pat, and again turning the butter through another 90 degrees.

4. A simultaneous slightly firmer pat to either of the 'short' ends of the oblong formed.

The process is repeated 4 or 5 times until a good geometric shape of a 'double cube' is achieved, roughly 6" x 3" x 3". A pattern of quiffs, tucks and crosses would be made on the top side for flourish and pride.

Even now in my head I can still hear the musical, slapping sounds of my mother's pair of Scotch hands…"dee-dee, dum, dum, **dum**…. dee-dee, dum, dum, **dum**."

The rhythm is roughly equivalent to an *'Andante con moto'* musical speed, 4/4 beat pattern. This 'butter rhythm' is arranged as: '2 and, 3, 4 **1**, 2 and, 3, 4, **1**, 2 and, 3, 4, **1** '.

It is hypnotically etched on my brain. The taste of good farmhouse butter is a rare and wonderful thing today. Before I started school, it was my small chore to wrap the precious butter in greaseproof paper, and pack it all carefully into 2 large brown leather bags, with tough zip fasteners, ready to take to Leek butter market on a Wednesday morning. Also the eggs, in sheets of newspaper, three in each small parcel.

SCRAIGHTING. *v.* Scraytin' or Skrikin' - Crying. (see W.P.F., p.125.)

SCRANIL. *n.* Something inferior, weak, or of poor worth. Livestock or person!

SCRATCH. *n.* A low wooden bench, usually pine, used for slaughtering and butchering pigs on. Usually about 5 or 6 feet long, 2 or 3 feet wide, standing on four stout legs about 2 feet high.

SCRAWP. *v.* Scratch or scrape, especially of flesh wounds. "Ey wur scrawpped-up buth arms after 'edge-cuttin' o' dee." - He was scratched all over both arms after hedge-cutting all day.

SIDE. *v.* (Side-away) To clear the table of crockery, cutlery and any food. The request would be: "Side th'table away!"

SITHEE.- *Literally*, **"**See you! or look there!" A possible usage might be: "Nar sithee 'ere surrey!" – Now look here my friend, or, "Sithee! a fox!"

SHAPE. *n.* Sheep. (pronounced "Shaype" with an extended 'a' sound.)

SHEARLING. *n.* (Sharling.) A sheep that has actually been shorn once. Older than a *hogg*, which is an over- wintered lamb born in the preceding Spring.

SHEEP-COUPLES. *n.* Soft-iron neck collars, joined by a short piece of light chain, with a swivel in the middle, in pairs. Used on sheep 'to couple' them in twos, thus preventing trespass over walls. Unfortunately, sheep eventually get used to them after a while. It is a sight to behold, when a pair of 'coupled', or 'yoked-together' sheep, observing the sweeter grazing in the neighbour's field, get the knack of running up to the wall, clearing it, without the slightest suggestion of "Four faults!" or "You naughty sheep!" being uttered by their Shepherd. The practise is now discontinued with the advent of barbed wire fencing, indignant Animal Welfare lobbyists, and the rather dubious practise by some farmers of turning a blind eye to their flock's 'foot-rot' problem. *'Couples'* were possibly invented by Noah? (For further reading see *'Hopples.'*)

SHIPPON. *n.* A cowshed. Some claim the word meant a small barn, or was derived from 'Sheep-pen'. By comparison, cowsheds are known as a 'bartons' in the West Country and 'byres' in Scotland. Cattle market cowsheds are called 'lairage'.

SHONNA. *v.* Shall not. E.g. "A shonna duit!"- I shan't do it!

SILING. *v.* Raining very hard, e.g. " It were silin' it down wi' rain."

71

SIEVE. *n.* Often pronounced "Si" (as in 'sigh') The round metal vessel which used to sit on top of the milk churns in the shippons at milking time. There was a detachable pair of perforated discs in the bottom of the "Si" between which was placed a pad of cotton wool type gauze through which the raw, warm milk would pass through into the waiting churn. The milk was first drawn out of the cow's teats by 'clusters' using collapsing membranes inside metal liners, and then conveyed by suction into the milking units – again special, metal utensils with close-fitting lids.

Filled churns, (in my day holding 10 gallons,) would then be 'dandied' (see description) to the dairy for 'in-churn cooling' - a framework of hollow pipes through which cold running water was passed , which then slowly dripped down the outside of the churn. This was all before pipeline systems, milking parlours and bulk tanks.

SKEN. v. To view closely. To peer at or study something closely through narrowed eyes.

SKEN-EYED. *adj.* Squint-eyed; cross-eyed would be *'boss-eyed'*

SKEW-WIFF. *adj.* Crooked or askew, not properly aligned.

SLARTS. *n.* – Insults, slanderous gossip.

SLANG. *n.* A small piece of ground, often part of a larger area, that is identifiable by some feature, e.g. "There's a slang as gus down back 'o woods." or "Dunna gu inter that bottom slang as is a bit wet and buttery, tha'll gyet thi tractor fast.(stuck)"

SLOPSTONE. *n.* The (usually) gritstone sink that graced most kitchens in the area, before the advent of the vitreous enamelled ones. There are very few in situ nowadays. I left the original in place at "Sycamores", Earl Sterndale, covering it with a thin piece of wood, and used as a 'sunken' cutlery drawer. The better specimens had a draining area to one side. Most of these articles have either been broken up, or put in the garden for use as planters.

SLUTHER. *v.* To walk in a shambling way, dragging the feet, or slovenly not picking them up. Also, as in a roof in need of re-tiling, e.g. "All slates 'av sluthered off on one end!", or indeed any collapsing situation.

SMARMY. *adj.* Insinuating, ingratiating. *"'E were smarmin' round 'er."*- He was trying to get round her.

SMOOSE-HOLES. *n.* Small purpose built 'tunnels' through the bottom of stone walls. Nets or rabbit-hangs would be positioned on one side of the wall tight up against these holes. A few 'beaters' would gradually work their way in an ever-decreasing fan-shape towards the holes, driving the rabbits or hares towards the 'open' ends of the *'Smoose-holes'*.

The game, or vermin, being used to using such 'runs' through the walls regularly, would then be ensnared after passing through the bottom of the wall. Afterwards, the holes would be left 'open' for some weeks before the next 'drive' occurred.

SNEATH. *n.* Curved wooden handle for a scythe. (J.B., 1997.)

SNECK. *n.* **(or Snick.)** A door latch. (see J.B., 1997.) A five-part iron-made opener/fastener consisting of:

1. A full-hand-grip handle, fixed top and bottom, nailed to the door at about chest height, with a pivoted 'thumb-plate' on the top.

2. A connecting strip going through a small hole in the door-plank from the pivoted thumb-plate to a downward-curving finger-latch on the other side of the door.

3. On this other side, a thicker, horizontal, straight strip of metal, nail-pivoted at one end, running over the top of the vertically-moving finger-latch.

4. A wideish iron staple near the edge of the door holding captive the straight strip, the latter just projecting past the edge of the door. This staple allows just enough movement of the straight strip to be lifted by the finger latch on one side, or

the connecting thumb-plate on the other side, to lift the said straight strip and clear …..

5. The barb-shaped catch which is nailed to the door-jamb and holds the straight strip secure, and therefore, by which the door is kept shut. Or else, the straight strip may be lifted clear of this catch, as just described, and the door opened.

Any Solicitor will understand and interpret this aforesaid schedule. Whereas and whether they could inasmuch and be tantamount to operate the said mechanism in the emergency of a fire at such said hereditament is debatable.

SNEEPED. *v.* Having one's nose pushed out. The doleful, lachrymose air worn by the child that is temporarily out of favour with the other playmates. Even describes the timid adult shouted down in the pub. (J.B., 21st. April, 2008.)

SNIED. (or Snided) *adj.* Thronged with people. e.g. "It were snided-out wi' folk!" (J.B., 21st April, 2008

SOHAM. *Prop.n.* Pronounced Sawm (or Sawms) The small hill behind Glutton Grange. The flat land on the north side of this hill is conjectured by some to be the site of a lost mediaeval settlement. This name is the earliest record of a place, or field that I have found in the parish of Earl Sterndale.

It occurs in *'Place Names of Derbyshire'* Part II, by Kenneth Cameron (published 1959), English Place Name Society, Vol.XXVIII, for 1950 -51, C.U.P., we have a reference to: SOHAM (lost), Salham 1086 D.B. (Domesday Book), *Salvin* (for *Salum*) 1244 FF, *Salme* 1415 *DuLaMB*, *Grenesalme* 1417 MinAcct, *Soham* 1830 Field Rate.

Possibly 'at the willows', v. salh (dat.pl. *salum*), -um.

The Lysons (*Derbyshire*, published 1817) were therefore correct in identifying this lost D.B. p.n. (place name) with a pasture in Hartington which they call *Saum*. No plan was available to the 1830 Field Rate, but from the position of the names it was apparently situated between Glutton and Fernydale. (English Place Name Society, 1959 C.U.P.)

74

SOUGH. *n.* (NB. pronounced "suff") - A drain. Therefore 'suffin'-rods' are yard-long bamboo (later plastic, - ugh!) rods joined up by brass screwed ferules for liberating blocked drains.

SOURGUTS. *n.* A weed, Swine grass. Short and stubby, with carmine-red flower spikes.

SPALCH. *v.* Split a bit off a piece of wood, either by accident or intention.

SPELL. *n.* A wafer-thin piece of softwood for lighting a candle from an open fire, or from candle to candle. (see S.P., p.66.)

SPROTTLE. *n.* Trying valiantly, but not really getting anywhere. "Worrat sprottlin' at?" - "What are you trying to do?" Could be applied to this book.

SQUAB. *n.* A young pigeon, especially one still in the nest. (W.P.F., p.122.)

SQUITTER. *v.* Extreme diarrhoea in young animals. Especially young calves being over-fed milk whilst being bucket-reared. (S.P., p.67.)

STALE. *n.* *(Stail or Steel)* The wooden shaft that fits into a brush-head. (see S.P., p.67.)

STANGS. *n.* A pair of longish, wooden poles only as thick as could be easily gripped by one in each hand. On a small-holding that couldn't afford a horse, or on steep, difficult ground, at hay-making time, these poles were placed parallel on the ground, loaded with hay in the middle, then the 'stangs' would be picked up by two people, one at the front, one at the back, and the hay then carried to the barn.(S.P., p.67.)

STARVED. *adj.* very cold, through either frost or snow or heavy rain. - NOT through hunger. E.g., "Am starved death!" is actually – I'm frozen to death! Burial entries in old church records sometimes gave a cause of death as; "…starved to death." meaning perishing through exposure, rather than hunger. (S.P., p.67.)

As my grandfather would remark about housing sick animals inside a building out of the weather, or putting weakly lambs next to the fireside in a cardboard box: "A've niver seen nowt dee o'warmth!" – I've never seen anything die from warmth."

STEAN. *n.* (pronounced 'steen') A large, round, earthenware vessel, like a pot, usually salt-glazed, used for storage. (see *pancheon*). (S.P., p.67.)

STEENDER. *n.* The recent local name for Earl Sterndale.

STIRK. *n.* – A young heifer, around one year old.

STRING-HOLT. *adj.* To describe an animal that has strained a tendon in a back leg.

Sometimes after parturition (birth), or after a fall, an animal would sometimes lift a back leg unnaturally high with the tendons drawing the leg up towards the hip. Literally, it is the ham-string that is 'halted', - temporarily pausing the leg at a high point in the animal's gait. Often became more pronounced, pro rata, with quickening pace.

STRIPPING. *v.* Drawing the fore-milk from the cow's teats to check for mastitis, colostrum or any other problems. After the finish of each milking session, it was considered good practise to 'strip' the last few drops of milk.

With the increase in cow numbers that was the eventual 'much wants more' attitude in dairying form the 1970s onwards, there was not time to 'strip' cows in the stream-lined milking parlours. The practice occurred of spraying the cows teats with either iodine or chlorhexidine based solutions (with emollients to keep the tender skin supple) which acted as anti-bacterial barriers.

STRYNDALL. *Pron.* An early spelling of Earl Sterndale, in the Peak District (R.M. p.45) see *STEENDER* above.

SURREY. (Surry) Mate, Friend, e.g. "I'll tell you something mate, …" would be "Al tell thee what, surrey, …." I conjecture, as others do, it might have originated from '*Sirrah*' the medieval term for a subordinate - mentioned in Shakespeare's plays occasionally.

SWAY. *n.* The wrought iron arm that was fixed at the side of the open fire or cooking range. On it hung various pot-hooks of adjustable heights to hang kettles, stew-pots or griddle-irons from. The sway could be swung away from the fire at ninety degrees into the room, still pivoted in the stone sides of the fireplace to either add ingredients to, or draw the contents from.

SWILKER. *v.* Liquid swirling around in any receptacle. (see W.P.F., p.122.)

SWINGLE-TREE. *n.* The wooden, 'straight-banana' (?) - shaped piece that joins the two trace- chains either side and at the back of the working harness-horse. By a central hook on the other side of the Swingle-tree is attached to whatever implement is being pulled.

T

TAILING. *v.* A means of incapacitating a cow's ability to kick. Even when held in a 'cattle-crush' (a metal crate to hold an animal for any veterinary treatment or administrational purposes, e.g. ear-tagging, etc,) a cow can give a painful and dangerous kick. 'Tailing' is the act of raising the tail upward as far as it may go and holding it firmly there. This restricts the movement in the animals back legs considerably. A useful method for restraining newly-calved heifers during the first few times of applying the teat-cups of the milking clusters.

TARNACK. (Tarnock) *n.* A good-for–nothing, a wastrel or profligate.

TASSLE. *n.* A rascally person, one of poor character or idle propensities.

THA . You. "Tha'rt a rum un!" – You're a card!

THA-NOWST. You know. A composite word that either begins or is tacked on to the end of any sentence.

THAW-STONE EDGE. *n.* ("Thawst'n-edge", "Thawings", or "T'heelston.") The pieces of square-cut sandstone blocks, (later continuous lengths of concrete) about a foot wide, six to nine inches deep and a yard, or more, long that were laid at the back of the cow's bed or *'boose'. (see above.)* The cow's hind legs would stand on this area, enabling them to defecate into the lower *'groop'* *(see above.)* behind and below. 'Th'eelstons' had to be brushed off and kept clean during hand-milking times, also just before 'mucking-out' with the shovels.

THEE. You. Curiously not all people seem to link or really be aware of the Biblical connotation of this old-fashioned way of addressing each other. E.g. "Thee's non be trusted!" – You're not to be trusted. Could also be "Thas non be teken notice on" – "You're not to be taken seriously."

THICK. *adj.* (or "thick with".) Describes the special relationship between two people as observed by others. The phrase might be: "She's thick wi'im" – She is familiar with him. The saying 'As thick as thieves' concerns a clique of individuals.

THISTLESPUD. *n.* A wooden-hafted tool for grubbing out thistles by the roots. It had two short v-shaped tines which dug into the ground either side if the thistle stem and was then prised in a levering action to extricate the offending weed. Some types had a short blade on the other side of the tines to slash off obstinately tough ones. Scything was the other method. Chemical spraying is the only absolutely sure method of control, but there are areas tractors cannot access, knap-sack spraying then being the answer.

There is something perversely satisfying about scything thistles, I fear there is a bit of '*Culloden*' in every Englishman and a bit of '*Bannockburn*' in every Scot!

THRALLS. *n.* The large, square-cut slabs of sandstone horizontally placed up against and around the walls of most cellars. Built up on either brick or stone supports, they were really the first storage worktops. (T.H., Vol.6, p.255.)Used for storing salted-down meat, vegetables, or indeed any foodstuff to be kept cool and dark. Often had a hole about the size of a 'half-crown' coin drilled through them. When the meat, mainly pork, was 'salted–down' ready for the long winter months, the rough salt was spread all over the sides of meat. After each piece of meat was used, a bucket would be placed under this hole and the salt scraped towards the middle of each thrall, to trickle through the hole and into the waiting receptacle for re-use. Traditionally, women were not allowed to undertake the salting-down of pork, the superstition being that meat handled by a woman in her menstrual cycle could become tainted.

THREAP. *v.* Excessive, dogmatic, bullying argument employed by someone to unfairly deny or discount another

79

person's statement. - Usually uttered by the person being 'threaped!' E.g. "'Ee threap'd me out as it weren't raight!" – He wouldn't have it any other way but that he was right and I was wrong.

THROMPECK. *n.* (or Thrompet.) The 'omega'-shaped ring, about 4" to 6"diameter, which slid up and down the '*rodstake*,' (see above). This almost-complete circle of iron had a hinged slightly-rounded rectangle loop on one 'horn' of the 'omega' which completed the 'ring' when snapped over the other 'horn'. From this other horn the actual cow-chain was fastened.

To fix the appliance:

1. The 'opened' Thrompeck was first put around the *rodstake*.

2. The '*cow-chain*' was passed completely through the middle of the 'hinged loop'.

3. The same hinged loop was snapped over the opposite horn to complete the omega shape into a 'running-ring'.

THRONGED. *n.* Busy or over-stressed with work. Also, describing a largish gathering of people, e.g. "Wer thur meny theer?" (Were there many there?)... "Ay, eet wur fair thronged wi' folk." (Yes, there were a lot of people.) - (T.H., Vol.6, p.255.)

THRUTCH. *v.* Excessive heaving at any load or task. In men, a coarse display of dramatic effort of brute strength. In women, bombastic, over-fussy competitive dominance. The 'Queen Bee' syndrome. (T.H., Vol.6, p.255.)

THUNGE. *v.* Hit with a sledge-hammer, Also, *v.* , the crass action of an over-weight uncultured clod-hopper. Also a descriptive term for someone with little taste or culture.

TICKLING. *v.* Catching trout without rod and line. Just using your fingers and patience to ensure your lunch. A past-time only the initiated can really possibly appreciate. A truly great sport of those country people who view 'angling' as an expensive, unproductive, time-consuming relaxation by those who are not hungry.

'Tickling' trout with just bare fingers requires a great deal of patience. Working up stream, for obvious reasons – the fish don't 'sense' imminent danger, as trout always point upstream when 'at rest'. Working downstream lets the fish be aware of vibrations in the water.

You must feel gently among the tight roots of trees and reeds where trout are lying, also underneath large flat stones in the river bed. It is surprising what a tight nick in rocks and stones a trout may hide in. On first touching a wriggling trout it is an alarming sensation.

However, working gently from the tail end towards the head of the fish, the hand is slowly worked up the body towards the opening and closing gills. Stroking very gently, it is then possible to get the thumb and forefinger to quickly grip in the gill cavities. Too rashly, and the fish will simply slip through the fingers. Once one has mastered the art, a great deal of sport and appetite may be satisfied.

"Give a man a fish, and tomorrow he will still be hungry, teach a man to fish, and he will never be hungry."

TIDY. *adj.* A considerable amount, e.g. "It's a tidy way to York." – It's a sizeable journey.(T.H. p.305).

TIT. *n.* A horse. (and never regarded as coarse slang locally.) Some people insist it refers to a young horse that has been 'collar-broken' i.e. used for draught, but still under five years old. I wouldn't argue.

TOLT. *v.* Told. "Ar tolt 'im!" – I told him!

TOOTHRI. *n.* A few, several. Literally, two or three, but not exactly that number ! A nuance which has to be learnt by experience. (T.H., Vol.8, p.305).

TOWD. *v.* (pronounced toed, or toad.)– Told. "A towd 'im so!" - I told him so.

TROW. *n.* A trough.

TUMBRIL. *n.* A large, barrel-shaped, wooden vessel, mounted onto a cart which is filled with urine from a tank below ground level by a simple 'lift-pump'. This vessel is used for taking out and sprinkling urine collected by drains from in-wintered stock onto the fields for fertilisation. (Also used in the French Revolution as a final ignominious form of transport to public execution for condemned Aristocrats. - Strange how their blue blood became embarrassingly red after their necks had being kissed by Madame Guillotine.)

TUNDISH. *n.* A funnel.

TURNING EGGS. *v.* When keeping poultry for breeding purposes, it was the practice to collect the fertile eggs and store them temporarily before setting them in an incubator or under 'broody' hens. The eggs would be marked lightly with a pencil with an 'O' on one side and an 'X' on the other. They would then be placed, only one layer high, on a bed of bran, about half an inch thick, on large open dishes, holding perhaps 25 or 30 eggs. Twice a day the eggs would be gently 'turned' by hand, so that all would be either 'O' or 'X' to the top. Kept in a cool, dark place the eggs would lie in suspended animation until enough had been collected to be brooded and, hopefully, hatched. Eggs could be kept on bran in this way for up to two weeks . After that time, the fertility and hatching-out success diminished.

TWITCH. *n.* A short piece of rope attached around the upper lip of a horse and tightened with a short piece of wood twisted through it. Only used on a 'biter' or bad-tempered animal or one made so by an unsympathetic owner. Only used as a last resort when 'gearing up' to a cart or implement or when the animal was being re-shod.

P. Holland.

U

UMBLES. *n.* Offal. The heart, liver, kidneys, etc. of an animal. Reputedly the Lord of the Manor ate the best meat, leaving the poorer cuts and offal for the servants. "Eatin' 'umble pie" may well come from the word. To be contrite, servile or apologetic seems to fit the metaphoric eating your own words.

URCHIN. *n.* A hedgehog.

V

VARMINT. *n.* A bad character, a rogue. "'Ay's a varmint." – "He's a bad lad." I might conjecture the word possibly may have been a corruption of *vermin?*

VEXED. *adj.* Annoyed, angered by. Not quite the same nuance as 'a vexed question'.

The usage might be: "She wur proper vexed!" or "Well, I am vexed!"

W

WALL EYE. *n.* An eye, in an animal, that has no colour in the iris, some vision is impaired sometimes, sometimes not. A sheepdog with one is usually slightly cheaper to buy, but one of my best dogs had a wall eye, and was a brilliant dog.

WEAN. *v.* To take off milk, - to take suckling calves away from the cow, or take away lambs from the ewes.

WE'EN. Composite of 'We have'. E.g. "We'en done this, - we'en done that." - "We'en sheared todey."

WEN. *n.* A sebaceous cyst once commonly found on the scalp. Rarely seen today with the wonders of modern science.

WERNA. *v.* Composite of 'was not' (C.P. *p.3)*

WETHER. *n.* Male lamb, castrated soon after birth, reared for meat, usually sold within 12 months of age, but not always. Can be fattened slowly, dependant on breed and land quality. But usually slaughtered within 2 years to be economic. Obviously not kept for breeding. (ref: G.P.I. p.51)

WHEEL-BARROW FARMER. *n.* Derogatory name for a Small-holder.

WHETSTON'. *n.* A sharpening tool made from compressed carborundum about 12 inches long and 2 inches diameter, narrowing to both ends. (see 'Bullston').

WICKEN. *n.* (or Wiggin.) The Mountain Ash or Rowan. Local place names – Wicken Walls, Wigginstall. (see J.B., 1997.)

WIK. *adj.* (Or WICK) Sharp, alive, keen, wide-awake. Newly-born lambs that are vigorous, struggle quickly to their feet and suckle readily are described as 'wick'. (see also 'A few anecdotes' after "Z" below.)

WINDLES. *n.* The dry, unpalatable stalks of grass that have gone to seed. (see *pasture-topping).*

WISKET. *n.* A small basket for carrying produce, fruit, eggs etc., also a handled scoop, or small bucket, for measuring and feeding cattle cake, chicken corn, etc. (see T.H., Vol.8, p.305.)

WITTLE. *v.* To fret or be anxious. The nervous or worrying person so disposed would be described as a *'wittler'.* (T.H., Vol.6, p.255.)

WOES. *n.* Walls. e.g.. "O th'woes ar dairn." (All the walls are in bad repair).

There is the well-known tale of a new-comer to a Peakland village asking an old 'Local' what he did for work.

"Am a woer." came the reply.

"What does a 'woer' do?" came the second question.

"Well, a woer woes woes." (A waller walls walls.)

WOM. *n.* Home, e.g. "Am gooin' wom." - I'm going home.

WOODEN-TONGUE. *n.* An affliction occurring in cattle, The tongue becomes hard and lolls out of the mouth and swelling is noticeable under the lower jaw.

(N.B. - pronounced 'Wooden-*tong*, not *tung*)

WORRO. Hello! - probably derives from 'What-ho!'

WORRYBRAY. *n.* A wart. (see *Angleberry*) Usually growing on the undersides of cattle, more prevalent in summertime. Can grow as large as an apple, or more.

WRAITHES. *n.* The wooden side-pieces or frames fixed on a hay cart to hold the crop on in transport. (see T.H., Vol.8, p.305.)

WUN. *adj.* Wound up. "It's o' wun up!" – "It's all wound up." Could be applied to new mown grass wrapped tightly around an implement, or even someone who is excited or agitated.

X

The verb of asking is often pronounced as "Exed", e.g. "Didst ex 'im?" - "Did you ask him?" or "Ay exed mi" – "He asked me"

Y

YAR. Yes. "Yar yo an!" – "Yes you have!"

YAMMERING. *v.* (Yammerin' on) – Incessant talking, gossiping. (see C.P., p.5.)

YAFFLE. *n.* A Woodpecker.

YARL-UP. *n.* Vulgar, coarse shouting.

YED. *n.* Head. Insultingly, e.g. "Big-yed!", "Pot-yed!"

YELLING. *v.* Crying, sobbing.

YO. You. e.g.. "Yo munna duit." - You must not do that.

YOKES. *n.* The wooden, carved-to-fit-across-the-shoulders pole used to carry heavy pails or buckets . From either end of the yokes a pair of light chains hung down with hooks to attach the pails to. The yokes spread the load evenly over the back and shoulders, assisted by the hands on the bucket handles. I'm never convinced of the efficacy of yokes, their extra weight seems to off-set any ease of burden. But I suppose you could release your hands to blow your nose on a cold morning whilst still walking and working at the same time. 'Yokel' must derive from this word.

YOUN. (Yown) - You will, "youn 'affert gu." - You'll have to go.

YONDER. Over there, a long way away, the phrase would be "Weers 'arry?" -Where is Harry?" answer, "Ay's o'er yonder." – He's over there. Out of sight, usually.

YOWS. *n.* Ewes.

Z

No examples known – but I would welcome suggestions!!!!

I remember – I remember
Personal thoughts & tales of a hill-farmer

I remember –

'Timmy Ray's' and 'Syke's' fairs at Longnor Races and Hartington Sports... Walking to and from school... Two lots of near misses in Foot-and Mouth epidemics... Learning to drive a 'little grey Fergy'... The first 'Howard Rota-spreader'... Walking cattle at Spring 'turn-out' thirteen miles for 'summer lay' at Back-oth'-Brook... Digging sheep out of snowdrifts...

A milk jug covered with a circlet of muslin and hung with coloured beads... The rattle of the pitch fork on the pickin'hole door... Hollinsclough Silver Band at Jack and Hannah Wood's smallholding, 'Stannery', on Christmas Eve in the early 1950's... Ticklin' trout with my Dad and Frank Bagnall... The gentle 'hummering' of a sheep about to lamb... Young Farmer's Club... Burying a good old dog...

The pride of selling a good, newly-calved cow at Uttoxeter Market, and making it 'lucky'... Cowslips... The Harvest Festival Sale...

Kestrels... Cream on a churn... The smell of new hay... Birth in a barn, especially on Christmas Eve... Knowing it's all been done before - and hopefully it will all be done again...

Being custodian, for a short while, of something worthwhile... Close to nature, and the season's rounds. I'm glad that I lived through it all.

I helped my father to 'salt down' the last pig killed at Glutton Grange for home use in 1957. Bernard Smith of Jericho farm killed it, (quite illegally!) and my mother made interminable pots of 'brawn.' In my mind I can still see and taste the hams hung up in muslin down the back hallway on the old ham-hooks. The same salting-trough and the two stone cheese presses are still there today, but now in the garden at Glutton.

The last man I heard of using a 'Bonny-rake' (see definition or, to save time, it is a hand-pulled, metal-tined, wooden-handled tool smaller than the horse-drawn, two-wheeled hay-rake) was Bill Etches at Dowall in the early 1950s. The last time I saw a hayfield being scythed completely by hand was near Flash, around 1960.

I think I may be among one of the last in this generation to go scything thistles by hand, as recently as 2002! Though, to be fair, I could name one or two that still know what to do with a 'bull-ston', a 'sneath' and a 'patin'blade' - though Father Time knows there aren't many left.

The last time I saw corn being 'stooked' by hand was in a field near Chelmorton in about 1960. The last two people I remember 'raking-out' the corners of a hayfield with wooden hay rakes were; Alethea Nadin, of Glutton Bridge (for my father in the 'Horse Paster' in 1957) and my late, wonderful mother-in-law, Mrs. Ada Cartledge (at Sparrowpit in the late 1960s and 1970s). The last person I saw taking a churn of milk by road, hand-pushed on a 'dandy', down to Glutton Bridge cheese factory was Mary Brindley, at Underhill, around the early 1960s.

Stangs (see definition) - As a child, I remember seeing two women carrying hay on stangs near to 'The Eagle and Child' pub, near Gradbach. There was a local tale of two un-married, miserable sisters (described as 'fow-faced an' gettin' on a bit') who, had not been seen for a while. "'appen theev run off wi' stangs!" was the conjecture of a local wit.

March dust is worth a guinea an ounce – Meaning that the weather has 'picked-up', the heavy winter rains have eased, and there is enough warm wind to dry the plough field's soil into dust.

Scything thistles had its own particular jingle: **Thistle in May, you'll rue the day, thistle in June, you'll thistle too soon, thistle in July, your thistle will die.** (The timing was fairly correct).

When March has cum an' gone, snow 'l melt on a cowd ston' – this is self explanatory.

Faightin' an' scraightin' orlis gyets th'kyat 'i kittle - Fighting and crying always gets the cat pregnant! When couples quarrel, often a pregnancy occurs later. The metaphor to caterwauling felines is not far wrong.

Good hay never turns back - When hay is almost ready to be carted to the barn, a good test is to take a handful of it and twist it tightly. If it immediately untwists itself, there is still some moisture there. 'Good' or 'ready' hay will stay twisted.

Instead of labouring first and chatting later, an idle gossipy person might say **"We'll gyet us sittin' down done furst."**

There was a tale of a couple in their late nineties who tragically lost their only son (in his late seventies). The old father turned to his wife and commented sadly – **'Ar tow'd thee weesh'd niver rear 'im.'**

One particularly tight-fisted and miserable farmer used to call his sheep to the feeding troughs in winter-time, only to give them nothing. He said 'It's non what yer give 'em; it's th'excitement of cumin' t'th'trough.'

Another quaint old codger courted a lonely spinster for well over forty years. When she finally got the suspicion that he might want a bit of a push to 'pop the question' she said to him 'John, John, doant yer think it's abairt time as wey gyet marridt?' His reply was: 'Well, I do Martha....but who'd 'av us pair o' beggars at our time o' life?'

There is the true story, within living memory, of a farmer of the parish moving 25 miles away to a new farm in Staffordshire. One day he was 'belting' his sheep prior to shearing. (see definition) A neighbour's young lad came over to see what was happening. The farmer asked the lad 'Dunya belt yoer shape?' (Do you belt your sheep?) The lad, not knowing the dialect answered: 'Me dad won't let us hit anything with a stick.'

A fair few or a tidy few means quite a number, but never quantifiable!
A toothri' - means a few or several, literally two or three, but, surprisingly not exactly either of those numbers!

I remember old Bartle Bagshaw of Oak farm, in 1954, at a time when there were only five or six cars in Earl Sterndale. With his brown three-piece suit, brown leather leggings and boots and his big, brown trilby hat, brim turned down all the way round, he used to drive with his left foot over the clutch, right foot over the brake, left hand to steer and change gear, and his walking stick in his right hand on the accelerator! I think the car was the model known as an "Austin 16".

My father and grand-father, like anyone else, spoke in differing idioms in differing circumstances. But it was very pleasing when they met up with some of the 'older characters'. I would listen, fascinated, as they lapsed into the 'old' ways of speaking. People like Jack and Hannah Wood at Stannery, Charlie Melland, Abe Watson, Charlie Hodgkinson, Civil Stone, Miss Kidd, 'Banty' Bagshaw, Mrs. Hall from the Post Office, Mrs.Wheeldon at Dove Cottage, Luke Gregory, 'Chummy', Miss Finney, Charlie Slack, Ted Heathcote the school caretaker, Walter Mellor at the 'Quiet Woman' pub and Tommy Percival, who used to walk round the area delivering the Sunday papers! All wonderful characters and certainly every village was full of them once.

It was curious how all the farmers were called by their Christian names, followed by 'at', then finally their abode, but minus the word 'farm' or 'grange'. Harry Hodgkinson from Harley Grange would be simply ''arry at 'arley' or Bill Etches from Dowall Hall became 'Bill at Dower.' Others were: 'arry at Breemer, Bill at Dale, Frank at Glutton and so on. The 'tag' didn't just apply to the immediate vicinity: all farmers knew 'who was where' easily up to a radius of ten or twenty miles, or even more.

One of my favourite phrases was often bellowed by my father at the foot of the stairs on many very early mornings: **'Well a niver did upon mar wurt, ligging theer, an yo arner airt o' bid yit, youn ayther 'a fert' arter, ar ils youn 'affert' flit!'** ('Well I never, my word, lying there, and you're not even out of bed yet, you'll either have to alter, or else you'll have to go!' He was mimicking somebody else's phrase - sadly, I've forgotten whose.

There are plenty of omissions, and some contentious words in this dictionary of mine. I call it 'concise' because a study never finishes: it can always be added to. However, this is my own particular one - not definitive or even comprehensive - but it is an effort to record and preserve a regional, and a small one at that, way of speaking which, becoming used less and less is in danger of being lost. Whereas the modern English Dictionary has many new words added to it each year, my Dialect Dictionary is conversely shrinking fast as the 'old ones', who still speak some of it, die out. There were only a few that spoke totally in a truly dialectic language - Charley Melland and Charlie Hodgkinson spring to my mind, but I cannot think of a single person now who does.

At the beginning I should have greeted you with;
Ay up, surrey, owart? - Hello there, friend, how are you?
And I will finish now with –
A moun mek tracks fer wom, al sithee! – I must go home, I'll see you!

Words, Spelling and Pronunciation

They have no thunder in their speech, or crashing of the teeth, like the lower Britons in France; they speak not in the throat like the Welch; they have no querolous tone like the Irish, no grave tone descenting in the fall like the Scotch, no wharlting like them of Carleton in Leicestershire, but something a broad language like the Dorick dialect in Greek

Philip Kinder's *Prolusion* to *Booke of Derbieshire*

Derbyshire born, Derbyshire bred, strong i'th' arm, an' wik i'th' yed is a jingle often recited. Some people say that '*wik*' means weak. Let me assure you that nothing could be further from the truth. '*Wik*', or '*wick*', to give another spelling, means sharp, shrewd, canny, astute, and not to be underestimated. When a farmer describes new-born lambs as being '*wik*', it means they are strong, healthy and able to thrive, even in the harshest of Derbyshire's Springtime.

There is a third meaning to '*wik*'. To find out, we could eavesdrop on a typical meeting between two old farmers, both born within earshot of Earl Sterndale Church bells:

Bill: Ow art, surrey? I 'anna seed thee fer **wiks!**

Tom: Am oraight, airt thee?

(**Wiks** here obviously means 'weeks').

The word '**surrey**' is generally accepted as being a corruption of '*sirrah*' by most linguists and language experts. The Concise Oxford English Dictionary describes it as:

"sirrah /`sira/ n. *archaic* = Sir (as a form of address)

[probably from Middle English *sire* Sir]" (The Concise Oxford Dictionary, p.1297.)

Certainly, '*sirrah*' occurs in many of Shakespeare's plays on numerous occasions; for example in King Lear, 1.iv. 114, when the Fool says to Lear:

Fool: 'Sirrah, I'll teach thee a speech.' (Shakespeare, p.1080.)

In David and Ben Crystal's book *Shakespeare's Words* the authors give the nuance of the word in this context as: [familiar] - (Crystal, p.9).

Back to the two farmers speaking in dialect:

Bill: Tha's non *turned inter editch* yet.
Tom: Non yit, … mind *thee, backend's comin'*, Ar sh'll aff *shape mi'sen*.
Bill: '*Ast* a *thrompet* or two *spare mi?*
Tom: Aye, Av gyet a *toothri* i' th' *stirk shippon*.
Bill: *Sithee!* Theer gus *th'ern*.
Tom: Ee's *borsend* wi' *trairt* frum *th'bruk!*'

Translation: (especially for European Ministry of Agriculture Officers in Brussels)
Bill: You haven't put your cattle into the secondary growth of grass yet?
Tom: Not yet. Mark you, Autumn's coming, I must make an effort.
Bill: Have you got any cow-chain fastenings you could lend me?
Tom: Yes, I've got two or three in the young-stock cowshed.
Bill: Look (you)! There goes the heron.
Tom: He's fat with trout from the river!

By comparing the two sections line by line and also with the generalized section below, we may get a clearer insight into the complexities of language and nuance

To put the above into Official Euro-Subjects-Speak:

Bill: Farming grazing terms and management practices.
Tom: Seasonal reference and independent personal awareness.
Bill: Specialist bovine equipment, borrowing requirements.
Tom: Numerical accounting, juvenile cattle accommodation.
Bill: Visual health and observation of protected species.
Tom: Dietary indulgence, piscatorial and environmental issues.
All communicated by words and syntax - nothing too challenging for Brussels there then. Now we may begin to appreciate the sweet simplicity of dialect!

As explained above, the Derbyshire word for the building which houses cattle is a *shippon*. In an article in *The Reliquary*, The Right Hon. Lord Denman writes:

' *"Shippen"* is the old English word for a small barn; it is to be found in Bailey's Dictionary, published in 1731, and traced to the north country: it is in constant use in Derbyshire." (Denman, 1862 -63, Vol.3, p.114.)

The two farmers continue:

Bill : Them *noo folk exed* if they cud *ley thur tit* wi' me.
Tom: Tha munna put 'osses ont' *belland*, th'll *dee!*
To clarify:
Bill: Those commuters have asked me if they can graze their horse on my land.
Tom: You musn't put horses on land contaminated with lead, they'll die!

Lord Denman also comments on this unfortunate aspect of one of Derbyshire's ancient industries, lead mining:

"Belland. Lead. A complaint caused by eating or imbibing vapour, or particles of lead, on grass or in water."(Denman, 1862 – 63, Vol.3, p.116. or Appendix 2, p.5)

Though lead mining has long disappeared from Derbyshire, in my recent local questionnaire to almost 150 people between the ages of 88 and 9 years, *Belland* was a word that all the people in the upper half age group still knew.

Spellings of all dialect words are fraught with problems. I try to write them as phonetically near to the pronunciation that I know. As an example of the required sound that may hopefully be understood by the phonetic spelling, I offer the word:

Clusummed (clusumpt), which could be phonetically spelt

"Kluzhmd" or "Kluzumpt",

It means clumsy through hands being cold in winter - chapped hands or mild frostbite.

Kl	uz	hm	d	(pt)
Hard C&L/	as in buzz/	humming sound/	plosive d	(or pt)

Some of the main features of Derbyshire dialect pronunciation are: the deep *'U'* sound; the dropping of *H* at the beginning of words; using *t'*, or *th'*, for the article 'the'; keeping the archaic *'Thee'* as the form of address, the omission of many *'L'*s and also other consonants in the middle of words; and using composite words which may stand for a longer phrase. In verbs, mainly all end *'ng's* are not pronounced, e.g. 'wonder*ing*' would be pronounced 'wundrin'' and 'work*ing*' would be 'wurkin''', i.e. no nasal *'ng'* sound at the end.

There is a general tendency in Peak District dialect to omit words in a sentence - whether this is laziness or a desire to be a person of few words is a matter of conjecture. These composite words, i.e. where two, three, or even more are joined to make a longer conglomeration are a feature of the vernacular language, for example:

Fetchbeesewut? - Will you go and gather the cattle in?

As already stated, the Derbyshire '*u*' is pronounced with a deep, sonorous sound: *Ee'sgoneBuxton* (He's gone to Buxton) or *passbutterwut* (Pass the butter will you) i.e. not the halfway sound between 'Baxton' and 'Buxton', or 'batter' and 'butter' that can be heard in the Home Counties. It might be useful and interesting to drop the jaw low when speaking this vowel, to imitate the authentic sound.

The letter 'L' is one which is omitted is many words, for example: *co'd* for cold, and *to'd* for told. (Though these are often written as *cowd* and *towd*.) The other three letters in these two examples are pronounced in exactly the same way.

Meanwhile, our two farmers are still chatting:

Bill: *Wur* that *'ay* as tha *get* airt o'th' field *agen Crothcut* a bit *nesh?*
Tom: *Non* sa bad, it'll look better on't snow; *beese wunna* leave a *rissom* then!
Translation:
Bill: Was that hay that you harvested from the field against Crowdecote a bit soft?
Tom: Not too bad, it will be alright in winter, the livestock won't leave a scrap then!

The word *nesh* has two meanings

1. To describe hay that has been harvested without having had quite enough sun to sufficiently dry it out (the danger

98

may be that the produce can 'over-heat' in the barn. As it 'sweats out' the excess moisture, it may lead to a 'natural combustion' fire.

2. Describing the tender characteristics of someone who feels the cold easily, is prone to illness, or is generally not an outdoor type.

Lord Denman gives his first definitions as:
"Naish, sub.   Tender.
Naish, verb.   To make tender.
Naished it, v.n.   Shirked or avoided it from sensitiveness.
(Denman,1862-3,   p.116. or Appendix 2, p.5.)

Julie Bunting, in her 2008 article, gives this definition:
"Nesh is still familiar, derived from an Anglo-Saxon word meaning tender or soft and usually directed at someone who is sensitive to anything mildly unpleasant, especially cold weather." (Bunting, 21.04.2008, p.13.or Appendix 2, p.49.)

Lord Denman must have done further research, as all good students should, and gives a second rendition with some etymological anchorage:
'The word "naish," though occasionally so pronounced, was a mistake, for it is derived from nesc, the Saxon word tender; and therefore nesh is the more correct way of spelling it.'(Denman, 1863- 4, p.14 or Appendix 2, p.7.)

......(What was it Tom said to Bill about a *rissom?* Let's ask him).............

Tom: A *rissom?* nowt left *i'th' kratch*, non a bit o' *fodder* t'eet, *clemmed'eath.*

(A rissom? nothing left in the hayrack, not any hay to eat, Starved to death.)

Ah, so it means a morsel of cattle food?....or hungry?....a scrap?...or some hay?...or...? Perhaps we should read Samuel Pegge's book to get an mid-18th century definition:

Rissoms [riz-umz] of oats, sb. pl. broken sheaves, or straws with the ears.
[In the Peak, stalks or stems of corn with the ears intact] Obsolete.   (Samuel Pegge, p.59, or Appendix 2, p.15)

Obsolete? Did that mean people had forgotten it, or just didn't use the word anymore?

In Pegge's papers, collected up to1796, there was a grand total of 899 dialect words. When it was finally published exactly a hundred years later as *Derbicisms*, Thomas Hallam had already gone through it with a fine tooth comb in 1890. Hallam then produced a table, illustrating the gradual decline of dialect words over the hundred years from Pegge's death.

Words still in use ---------------------- 586
   "   obsolete ------------------------ 295
   "   doubtful if in use--------------- 5
   "   standard English-------------- 13

                     899

If Hallam maintained that the word *'rissom'* was obsolete in 1890, how can it be that the same word, and the only word, that 100% of the people who filled in my recent questionnaire knew the meaning of, was 'rissom'? Now, apparently, it means 'the least amount'.

I carried out a survey and questionnaire between 01.02.08 and 30.04.08 The questionnaire consisted of the knowledge of 36 random words of Derbyshire dialect. The same questionnaire sheets and questions were used throughout the survey.

People answering the questionnaire were between 88 & 9 years of age. The consent of the Officers of the Y.F.C. Clubs and Parents of Minors was obtained first.

Analysis of Survey & Questionnaire on Derbyshire Dialect.

PEOPLE & NUMBERS:

÷ Individuals residing in Earl Sterndale Parish all or most of their lives: **25**

÷ Members at *The Farming Life Centre* at Blackwell Hall, Taddington: **16**

÷ Buxton Young Farmers Club: **24**

÷ Bakewell Young Farmers Club: **35**

÷ Hope Valley Young Farmers Club: **38**

÷ Local N.F.U. & W.I. Members: **10**

Total: 148

Conclusion:

Effectively, at this rate of decline, the knowledge, hearing and using of dialect language in and around Earl Sterndale could virtually become extinct within 2 - 3 generations, or inside the next 50 – 60 years. (See diagrams)

Age Group	How Many	% of words known.
88 – 60 Years	30	100 %
60 – 40 "	26	45.37 %
40 – 20 "	20	21.38 %
20 – 15 "	32	16.35 %
15 – 10 "	30	7.52 %
Under 10 "	10	2.75 %

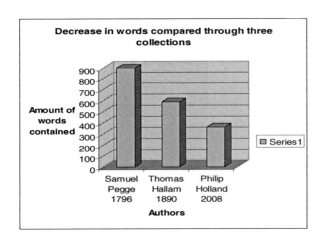

Our two farmer friends shake their heads:

Bill: Well, it'll be a ***rum do*** if'n we canna talk ***amonghand.***
Tom: ***Weesh'n*** 'af raight it dairn, ***ilse*** it'll o' be fergetten.

(Well, it will be a funny thing if we can't talk to each other.
We shall have to write it down, or else it will all be forgotten.)

(Pause)

Bill: ***Dus tha*** mean we'en ***af'fert*** goo University?
Tom: ***Ar,*** that Philip Holland's gone ***theer,*** 'an 'ees get no ***nous.***
(Do you mean we will have to go to University?
Yes, that Philip Holland has gone there, and he hasn't got any common sense.)

There's an embarrassed silence, as we sidle away...

Dialect is forthright, it is also compassionate, it can sound musical, and it can send shivers down your spine. It can make you wonder and it can make you laugh. It has some words and phrases which even Shakespeare and Dr. Johnson would be hard-pressed to better.

Whether your favourite figure of speech is ***flinkerin' wi'snow*** or ***as lesh as a pigtrough; hummerin' fer lambin'*** or ***as mowly as a cat turd,*** all this rich, quaint, simple and quirksome language is such an important part of our heritage and culture. It should be cherished and written down, listened to and spoken.

> *"Words from the heart that know not fear,*
> *to soothe, delight and charm the ear."*
> F. *Philip Holland.*

103

Derbyshire Historiographers & Lexicographers

Lexicographer. - A writer of dictionaries; a harmless drudge that busies himself in tracing the original, and detailing the signification of words.   Dr. Samuel Johnson, (1709 – 1784)

Samuel Pegge the Elder (1704–96), produced what is arguably one of the most comprehensive and authentic studies on Derbyshire dialect. One of the earliest county antiquaries is Philip Kinder (1597–1665), who compiled an initial extended synopsis entitled *Prolusion*, later transcribed and published by the Revd Dimmock Fletcher in *The Reliquary* in 1882 – 83. Though born in Sneinton, Nottingham, Kinder traces his unbroken genealogy back to 1385, to the Hayfield and Kinder Head area of Kinder Scout, (or Chendre, to give the ancient Celtic name). The family is noted in Lysons *Derbyshire*. My great-grand-mother was Sarah Kinder of 'Shireoaks', Hayfield, which probably explains my interest.

Lysons *Derbyshire* quotes Philip Kinder's book, and in two brief pages we are given a vivid insight into the lives and nature of Derbyshiremen; their lead mining, farming and dry stone walling; their wives, fashion and music; sport, pastimes, diet and dental state; and a list of the County's gentry and intellectuals residing there. It is a rare 'snapshot' of early 17th Century people's lives in a remote area. Interestingly, the word 'grooves', meaning lead mines, is mentioned. A 'groover' was a lead-miner.

One of the later influential literary men was Llewellyn Jewitt (1816-86). He started the *Derby Telegraph* in 1853, after which, interest in local history initiated him to found that eminent gentleman's periodical *The Reliquary* in 1860. But it is not until Gladwyn Turbutt's monumental, four-volumed *A History of Derbyshire*, published in 1999, that it is possible to say there is now, arguably, the most complete and exhaustive history of the county.

How fascinating it would be if we could listen to tape recordings of: the peasants in the Dark Ages, Plantagenet soldiers, 14th Century monks, Chaucer's or Shakespeare's companions, a sermon by John Wesley, or Dickens reading aloud. It would be a great loss if the heritage of dialect language were not recorded from time to time for both cultural posterity and future interest.

Language most shewes a man; speake that I may see thee
Ben Johnson, 'Discoveries', (1641)

Dialect Poems

Charlock
Ploughing, and the urge of Spring

"Youn 'af fert' flit!"
("You'll have to go") Recounting an old tale.

Buxton Market, 1913
After reading Thomas Hardy's '*The Breaking of Nations*'.

The Girl with Auburn Hair
A ballad - a true story.

Charlock. *
(Op.136, 08.12.07)

She dreams for a year, or ten, or more,
this simple, humble weed,
this teasing beauty,
this huckrel! *

And when we plough,
back she comes,
a feather-green shoot,
persistent now.
Kissed awake by lifting iron,
caressed by the coulter, spinning slow,
urged with the harrow's dance,
and rolled in the tilth, to grow.

And when we sow,
she is up already, drinking in the rain,
quivering in her wind-blown freshness,
her pale flowering again.

And when we frown,
she laughs, and sings her delicate scorn,
knows no denial of her children's children
yet unborn.

And when we mow,
she disappears,
with all her green and yellow,
and hides, and sleeps, and dreams.
Waits for a fanfare
of blundering hooves,
the next heave of the share*.

Who does not dream
of their lover's next kiss?
What harm
was there?

Charlock – *Derbyshire dialect for wild mustard (Sinapis arvensis), with pale yellow flowers. Also called field mustard. A weed of which the seed may lay dormant for many years, but will quickly germinate at any subsequent ploughing.*
Huckrel – *a Derbyshire dialect term for a young woman, if not of doubtful morals, then of questionable virtue.*
* **Share** – Shortened form of *ploughshare.*

Youn 'af fert' flit.

Ar niver did upon mar wurt!
Yo arner airt ter bid,
liggin' theer o' of a peece.
Youn ayther 'af fert' arter,
or ilse Youn 'af fert' flit!

> Thees God gi'en daise,
> Well shall thi waiste?
> Win o'oth' hee is cut an' swotht,
> wints teddin' airt tuth' braize,
> An' dawn thar's yit fert' taiste.

Tha's bin airt o' nayhts
A'cortin' rairned abairt.
A slattern huckrel th'as fund thi'sen.
tha'll mek thi bed, an' lie thi dairn,
But non bi'us ar dairt!

> 'Appen tha's geyt er foaled 'ast?
> Tha'll not be fust ort' last.
> Win lads ar' men thi louws
>   thur'sen,
> an' trouble follers on.
> Geyt thi up, an' fast!

Cum thi dairn tha mucky arse!
Th'daise aif gon fer thay.
Tha'll swet thi trouble airt i'th sun,
tho tha's up an' fired thi gun!
ilse flit thisen t'dee!.

> Yar, mi lad, tha'll smart sum
>   mower,
> Win th'Justice co's thi shame.
> Thi huckrel's dead,
> I'th wurk-hise bed,
> thi chance-childt's geyt thi
>   name!

Wots this, mi lad, ay nay!
thart 'ingin 'igh by th'rope!
An' it's scraight ar must,
i'th heefayld's dust
Tha'rt dead, an' that's no 'ope.

Cum thi dairn, mi lad,
Th'art stiff all o'er, an' gree.
A'l kape thi chance-childt,
Cum what may,
Tha's flit, an' arl rue t'dee.

Translation:
Circa 1850: An old farmer angrily calls his son to get up. He
knows that his son has got a girl into trouble, and has just
found out she has died giving birth in the workhouse. He
enters his son's bedroom to find that he has committed
suicide.

You'll have to go.

Well I never, upon my word!
You're not out of bed,
lying there altogether.
You'll either have to alter
or else you'll have to go!

These God-given days
will you waste?
When all the hay is cut and lying in
rows,
wants *tedding** out to the breeze,
(fluffing up to dry)
and dawn you haven't yet tasted.

109

You've been out at nights
courting round about.
You've found yourself a sluttish tart.
As you make your bed, you'll lie on it,
But not in my house I doubt!

                            Perhaps you've got her pregnant,
                                         have you?
                            You're not the first, or the last.
                            When boys become men they
                                      lose themselves,
                            and troubles follow.
                            Get up, be quick about it!

Come down, you dirty arse!
The day's half gone for you
You'll sweat it out in the sun
Though you've got her pregnant,
Or else move out today!

                            Oh yes, my lad, you'll smart some
                                       more
                            When the Magistrate calls you to
                                      book.
                            Your tart's died
                            in the workhouse,
                            your bastard's got your name.

What's this, son...oh no!
You've gone and hung yourself!
Now weeping is all I will do
in the hayfield's dust
You're dead, and now there's no hope.

                            I'll cut you down,
                            You're stiff and grey
                            I'll keep your baby
                            Whatever happens,
                            You're gone, and I'll rue today.

Buxton Market, 1913
(Op.143, 04.02.08)

They drive to market; down from the quiet, distant hills,
their panniers weather-bleached and filled with cooling bread,
The piebald, half-legged cob* uncomplaining in its dull-
hooved clops,
spinning fellies, creaking elm and slapping leather straps.

Martha, up before the sun, has tied her hair in ribbons,
half-heartedly completed when seen and held to scorn.
These, her yellow secrets, bought with last week's haggled
coins,
which false complaints about her wares her honest purse
depleted.

Her dour husband, caring little, and his temper never long,
always eager for the barrel-house, stops once along the way,
and finds his stick, ditch-left and lost the week before.
Young William cries the whole, full, fractious morning,
nurdling*, with his hand held to his ear,
his wooden toy denied, a slap received.

The town is reached, already humming at its trade.
Crowd all churning, milling, shouts of "two-a-penny!"
Stalls and canvas, loaded choice for nodding heads.
Bonnets, boots, black shawls and waistcoats bright with
chains.
People chaffing, jostling in the hive of barter,
Gostering* at last week's bargains,
winked, and now half price;
a fool is he who never learns.
Impatient cattle, fly-frabbed and whisking, stand and wait,
or stamp to the cobble's dusted heat,

111

sweat smelling, muzzle-dripped and tired.
A group of women gather round a wild-eyed zealot,
who calls "The End is Nigh!", his shaking hand held high.
A trader simply mutters, "*Ar, b'non till th'sun's gone dairn!*" *
and grins at his neighbour's groaning, still-stacked board.

But finally her bread is sold, the counted coins twice-checked
and changed for this week's bag of flour, fine-sieved and
snowed.
The disappointment still to come, when sadly split on
reaching home.
Young William stares, then starts and winces for the dozing
cob,
his father's stick hard struck, and better never found.

Martha, weary, looks towards the gathering storm,
climbs the float's warped, wooden tailboard,
and notices her hands, so worn, and raw, and old.

* ***cob*** – horse
* ***nurdling*** – whimpering
* ***gostering*** – staring stupidly
* ***Ar, b'non till th'sun's gone dairn*** - *"Yes, but not until the sun
has gone down!"*

THE GIRL WITH AUBURN HAIR
(Op. 14, 27.08.03. 100L)

for my Mother
(Written in broadest Staffordshire Moorlands accent of The Manifold Valley
Read phonetically is probably the easiest way)

'A tell ov a mayd frum th'village grayn*,	*green*
Agnes Pickrin' wur 'er naym.	
Born at a farm 'neyth an 'ill cow'd Shayn,*	*called Sheen*
An' 'oud gyet* orbun 'air.	*she had*
Oh shay wur fair, theer's none denay*,	*deny*
But wildt an' free, non fancy.	
Yit th'uther wenches made 'er cray*,	*cry*
An' taysd*_abairt 'er 'air.	*teased*
Th'yong men o' frum rind abairt*,	*around about*
Tray'dt the best fut win 'er.	
B'shay wur chusy, wi'airt a dairt,	
An' stalldt 'em wi"er stare.	
A'th'village Wakes thay danced 'er rairnd,	
'Er eyes wur o' a-sparklin',	
Win lads exed* tek 'er whum*, 'er frairnd,	*asked *home*
An' shuke that orbun 'air.	
Win Agnes grew ter womanhood,	
'Er Mother towd 'er then,	
As shay wur born o' chance-childt* blood,	*an illegitimate*
An' th'Feyther, none knew where.	

Then th'uther wenches spiteful wur,
When it gyet airt ont' gossip,
Thay turndt the backs an' laughed at 'er
Sed, "Cut yer orbun 'air!"

Well, Agnes back t'th'farm 'er ran,
An' tearful, sobbed an' crayed,
Shay exed 'er Mother "Wheer's the mon,
"Give mey this orbun 'air?"

'Er Mother's face then fell o' gray,
Shay bit 'er lip i'shame,
"A gypsy lad, wi' mey did lay,"
"An' ey 'ad orban 'air."

Agnes ran airt on t'th'ill,
An' 'id among o' rocks.
Shay 'eaved 'er 'eart wi' scraitin'* still,   *crying
E'en th'shape* were watchin' there.   *sheep

Er' lay theer thinkin' "What's ter cum?
"Who'll luke at mey frum nair?"
"A'l 'orn it*, though, what's done is done,"   *I'll put up with it
"Fer mey, ar nothin' care."

Neyht drew in, an'th'moun full rose,
Yit still 'er lingered theer,
Shay fell inter a fritful doze,
An' dreemt o"er feyther's 'air

Well, darkness passed, an' dawn cropt* in,   *crept
Shay wok up wi' a start.
'Er shivered wi' 'er frock sa thin,
An' damp 'er orbun 'air.

114

Then Agnes run frum offa th'ill,
Cross th'pasters* dewy sward   *pastures
Th'valley filldt wi' mist o' still,
A saight o' beowty rare.

Shay crossed thro' th'edge, an' int't'lane,
Then stopped, surprised ter sey,
A yong mon, leading 'orse an' wain*,   *cart
An' whistlin', wi'out a care.

"Na' then, lass, what's up?" 'ey axed,
"Tha lukes a bit upset,
Wut'na* tell, ar't sad?, or vexdt*?   *Won't you?   *angry
Tha's gyet sich pretty 'air!"

Shay gloppendt* wur, 'er body shuke   *dumbstruck
'Ey 'eld 'er wi' 'is eyes,
An' neyther brok their knowin' luke,
Su silent, buth did stare.

'Ey fexed* 'er kindly in 'is gaze,   *fixed
An' waited till shay'd calmed,
"What's thi name?, wheer gu thi ways?,
Swait* lass wi' orban 'air!"   *sweet

"Agnes Pickrin', frum Shayn 'ill,"
'Er answerdt, blushin' bright,
"Br'av* gyet many troubles still,   *But I've
A'm non abairt t'share."

Th'yong mon quickly took 'er 'and,
An' tender 'eld it theer,
"A trouble shared's a trouble banned,"
Ey sed, wi' voice o' care.

"Gyet they ont' cyart, a'l tek thi wom*,   *home
Albert'Holland, that's mi name.
Well o'er river's weer* ah'm from,   *where
On't Glutton* side o' wair*."   *(a village)   *weir

'Ey tuke 'er back t'er mother's place,
An lifted 'er dine* frum th'cyart,   *down
'Ey gazed inter 'er pretty face,
An' stroked 'er orban 'air.

"A'l cum an' sey thee, once i'a while,"
'Ey sed, "if tha dusna' mindt."
Shay niver spok, b'give a smile,
That niver smildt sa fair.

Thay courtdt all o'th'summer long,
As th' yong 'uns orlis* do,   *always
Till at last, theer love sa strong,
A ring were blest to wear.

Su* Albert n'Agnes 'appily wed,   *So
Thay lived at 'Stannery',
O'er fifty yeer, wur their homestead,
The good an' bad to share.

I'mey*, theer*_blood flows wharmly still,   *In me   *their
Ah'm* proud ter tell thee nair*,   * I'm   *now
Me* Great- grandmother, off Shayn 'ill,   *my
That lass wi' orban 'air.

This is a true story. Agnes Pickering was born 1850, baptised
19th August, at Sheen Church in the same year. Her mother
was Ellen, father not recorded.

Agnes was described as "...dairymaid, living with Grandfather," in the 1881 census. Her grandparents were William and Esther Pickering who farmed at High Sheen Farm, Sheen, Staffordshire.

Agnes married Albert Holland and they celebrated their Golden Wedding at "Stannery", Glutton Bridge, Derbyshire. Albert died 1937

Agnes died 1947, having held her first Great-grandchild, Joan Critchlow Holland, my sister, a few weeks before she died, 97 yrs old.

Genealogy

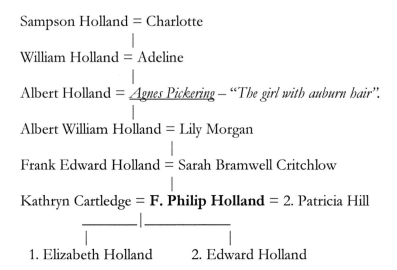

Sampson Holland = Charlotte
|
William Holland = Adeline
|
Albert Holland = *Agnes Pickering* – *"The girl with auburn hair".*
|
Albert William Holland = Lily Morgan
|
Frank Edward Holland = Sarah Bramwell Critchlow
|
Kathryn Cartledge = **F. Philip Holland** = 2. Patricia Hill

    1. Elizabeth Holland   2. Edward Holland

The first four Holland men, mentioned above, are all buried in Earl Sterndale Churchyard. William Holland was married three times and is buried with two of his widows, and one of his daughters, in the bottom left-hand corner of the graveyard, midway round the wall between the school and the churchyard gates. Sampson and Albert William and their wives are buried just left of the path way from the churchyard gates towards the tower.

Frank Edward Holland was cremated and his ashes are on Parkhouse Hill. There is a bronze memorial tablet to him at the foot of the 'Sugarloaf' rock, at the north-west end of Parkhouse Hill, erected there by his family.

F. Philip Holland has made it known he wishes cremation, and his ashes to be scattered on Parkhouse Hill also.

Bibliography

Byne, E. & Sutton, G. (1966) *High Peak*. London, Martin Secker and Warburg Limited.

Daniel, C. (1982) *A Diagnosis of Derbyshire Dialect*, (Article in March Ed., Vol.47), Derby, Derbyshire Life & Countryside.

Denman, The Rt.Hon. Lord. (1862) *A Fragment on the Dialect of The High Peak*. (Article in Vol.3), London, *The Reliquary*.

Dimmock-Fletcher, W.G. (1882- 83) *Transcription of Prolusion* (by Philip Kinder) London, The Reliquary.

Featherstone, W.P. (1978) *Notes on Dialect in the Dove Valley Area*. (Article in *'Derbyshire Miscellany'*, Vol.8, Part 4.) Derby, Derbyshire Archaeological Society.

Gilchrist, R. M. (1948) *The Peak District*. London, Blackie & Son Limited.

Innes-Smith, R. (1991) Ed. *Derbyshire Guide*. Derby, Derbyshire Countryside Ltd.

Kinder, P. (Hand-written around 1660*) Booke of Darbieshire*, MS Ashmole.Vol. 788, Duke Humfrey's Library, The Bodleian Library, Oxford.

Kinder, P. *The Prolusion*, in The Gell Papers, (D258/55/8), Matlock, held in Derbyshire Record Office.

Lawrence, D. H. (1964) The Complete Poems of D. H. Lawrence (Eds. Vivian de Sola Pinto & Warren Roberts), London, William Heinemann Ltd.

Lawrence, D. H. (1948) *The Complete Tales of D. H. Lawrence*, London, William Heinemann Ltd.

Lysons, D. & S. (1817) *A Topographical & Historical Account of Derbyshire*. London, Printed for T. Cadell and G. & A. Greenland by A. Strahan.

Milward, R. (1986) *A Glossary of Household, Farming and Trade Terms from Probate Inventories*. Chesterfield, Derbyshire, Derbyshire Record Society,.

O'Sullivan, M. (1997) *Early Derbyshire Historians, 17th – 19th Centuries*, Matlock, Derbyshire, Derbyshire County Council.

Pegge, S. (1896) *Two Collections of Derbicisms.* (Published for The English Dialect Society) Oxford, O.U.P.

Raistrick, A. & Jennings, B. (1953) *A History of Lead Mining in the Pennines.* London, Longmans

Smith, M. (1993) *The Spirit of The High Peak.* Ashbourne, Landmark Publishing Ltd.

Turbutt, G. (1999) *A History of Derbyshire.* (4 vols.), Cardiff, Merton Priory Press Ltd.

Wright, P. (1975) *The Derbyshire Drawl.* Clapham, Lancaster, The Dalesman Publishing Company Ltd.